# A STRATEGY
# FOR THE
# CHURCH'S MINISTRY

by

## JOHN TILLER

Chief Secretary,
Advisory Council for the Church's Ministry

CIO PUBLISHING
Church House, Dean's Yard, Westminster, London SW1

**ISBN 0 7151 2539 7**

Published September 1983 for the Advisory Council for the Church's Ministry by CIO Publishing.
Reprinted June 1984.

Printed by The Ludo Press Ltd, London SW18 3DG

# Foreword

Since 1978 the Advisory Council for the Church's Ministry has discussed some aspect of ministerial strategy at each meeting. In November 1981 it was decided to ask the Chief Secretary, Canon John Tiller, to produce a report which would have the unity of one person's view and also take into account the various discussions which have taken place. He was asked to complete his work, which had to be fitted in with other duties, if possible in time for a debate in the General Synod in November 1983.

The intention has been to provide a following debate to the one which took place in November 1980 on the report of the Ministry Co-ordinating Group, *The Church's Ministry—A Survey* (GS 459). That document was concerned to supply members of the newly-elected Synod with an up-to-date account of existing policy on various matters connected with the ministry, but the final chapter looked forward to the development of an overall strategy for the future:

> 'The Synod, for its part, needs to be alive to a dual responsibility–the need to make adequate provision for the Church's ministry in the period immediately ahead, and the need to be open and responsive to new forms of ministry bearing in mind that major changes invariably take a long time–possibly a generation–to work through.'[1]

ACCM hopes that the material provided here will stimulate and assist the Synod in discerning an appropriate strategy for the future which is responsive both to the needs of society and to the developments which are taking place in new forms of ministry. The views of the Council are being published as the official report to which Canon Tiller's work will be attached. But the need for strategic thinking is not something which is confined to the General Synod alone, and it is hoped that this wide-ranging survey will be made use of throughout the Church as a means of coming to grips with the issues which must be faced if there is to be effective strategic thinking and planning at every level.

RONALD PORTSMOUTH
Chairman
Advisory Council for the Church's Ministry

[1] *The Church's Ministry—A Survey,* GS 459, CIO, 1980, p.32.

# Acknowledgments

In the course of gathering material for this report over a period of about eighteen months I find that I have received evidence of one kind or another from all except seven of the dioceses of the Church of England. In the process I have become indebted to a wide variety of people, far too many to mention here by name. They range from a study group of clergy in rural Northamptonshire to a deanery synod in South London; from a Church Army officer who took me round a housing estate in Liverpool to a suffragan bishop who spent time in my office analysing his ministry in response to my questions. Many have given generously of their hospitality as well as their time: I have talked to bishops' wives in their kitchens, to a chaplain in the canteen of a college of technology, to an archdeacon in his study, to a priest-worker in his car, and reflected on what they have said in the quiet haven of St Francis' Retreat House, Hemingford Grey. To all these, and many more, I am profoundly grateful. The impressions I have gained of course remain impressions and I alone am responsible for the interpretation I have placed upon them. I have looked at new forms of ministry (e.g. an eldership team in Somerset, a full-time lay pastor in Kent) as well as more traditional approaches to contemporary problems of ministry (e.g. a united benefice in Herefordshire; a deanery chapter in inner-city Manchester). In no case was what I saw necessarily typical of what was happening elsewhere in that area, but I have, through the generosity of those concerned, seen something of what is going on and have tried to use it to think creatively about the future.

The Advisory Council for the Church's Ministry has displayed an alarming trust in my sense of proportion by commissioning me to undertake this work, and I have no doubt fulfilled the worst fears of its members. In spite of this they have never failed to support and encourage me, and while presenting it to the General Synod as what it is, namely one man's piece of work, they have nevertheless done much more to call for its serious consideration than would have been achieved by a distant 'what he has written he has written'.

There are four persons I must mention by name. With my Chairman, Bishop Ronald Gordon, I have enjoyed in this as in all things the best of working relationships. Both he and my theological consultant, Dr Peter Baelz, Dean of Durham, have been more than generous with their time: they have frequently gone out of their way to fit in with my programme when it should properly have been the other way round. Neither of them have ever pressed their own point of view, yet I have gained immensely from the wisdom and perception with which they, and other members of the Council, have discussed what I have written. Frances, my secretary, has always succeeded in combining the right proportions of cheerfulness and carefulness to keep me going, and her skill with a word processor has given me great freedom to revise the text. To her, and to the whole ACCM staff, I am specially indebted for their willingness to relieve me of various tasks in order to get the work done.

The illustrations have been contributed appropriately enough by one of the hard-pressed parochial clergy about whom I write. To the Revd E. W. L. (Taffy) Davies I am greatly obliged for his skill in conveying lightly but effectively points over which I have laboured. Quotations from published works, including the New English Bible, the Good News Bible, the Book of Common Prayer and the Alternative Service Book 1980, are reproduced here with permission.

Finally I must acknowledge, though I can never repay, my debt to my wife and family, who for several months have endured the alternatives of my absence of body when away from home and my absence of mind when there.

# Contents

# INTRODUCTION
# AND SYNOPSIS

1. This investigation is concerned with the ministry of the Church of England for the period 1963–2023. It assumes that at the end of that time there will still be a Church of England–and indeed a planet Earth, a Church of God and a ministry of the Gospel! A span of sixty years has been chosen, firstly because it is not beyond the scale of time measured by individuals, and secondly because for strategic planning a period is required which is neither too short to permit, if necessary, implementation of change, nor too long to support the assumptions on which the strategy is based. In this instance we are concerned with twenty years of past history and forty years still to come, long enough to put into practice a strategy based on experience. Among the men and women who are at present in training for the ministry of the Church of England there are some who can expect to serve for the entire future period in view.

## FOLLOWING THE PAUL REPORT

2. It was in 1963 that Leslie Paul produced his report, entitled *The Deployment and Payment of the Clergy*, for the Central Advisory Council for the Ministry (CACTM). After four years as Chief Secretary to the Advisory Council for the Church's Ministry (ACCM, successor to CACTM), a position with special opportunity for an overall view of the Church's ministry, I have been invited to propose a strategy for the future. It is the first time since the Paul Report that the Council has commissioned one person to write a general survey of this nature. Its reasons for doing so are connected with a number of developments in the understanding and the practice of ministry, which have occurred during the past decade. These are described in Chapter 2. It needs to be said at once, however, that my concerns are both wider and narrower than those of Leslie Paul. They are wider, because the ministry of the whole people of God provides the foreground to my work, whereas for Leslie Paul it was only the background to a debate about the clergy. They are narrower, because what I say is restricted to a general strategy based on certain fundamental theological insights about ministry; it is not part of my brief to enter into detailed discussions about the payment and deployment of the stipendiary ministry. Since the Leslie Paul Report (and to some extent because of it) there has been set up the Ministry Co-ordinating Group (MCG) which brings together ACCM, the Church Commissioners, the Church of England Pensions Board, the Central Board of Finance, and those of the Archbishop of Canterbury's staff who advise on the clergy

deployment system known as the Sheffield quota. This combined group now initiates its own studies and reports in the first instance to the House of Bishops.

THE CONCERNS OF THE GENERAL SYNOD

3.   When in November 1980 the MCG presented a survey of the ministry to the General Synod it expressed the hope that 'the Synod, while getting to grips with the more urgent practical issues, will seek an opportunity to take a longer term and more speculative view of the way in which ministry may need to be exercised, not perhaps immediately but within the lifetime of the younger members of the present Synod and of young men and women now offering themselves, and being trained, for ministry.'[1] What is provided here is designed, in the first place, to give the Synod such an opportunity. It therefore picks up some of the specific issues in the area of ministry with which the Synod has recently been concerned. These include the development of a local ordained ministry, the place of lay elders, and the renewal of the diaconate. There have also been debates in the Synod about the initial training and continuing education of the Church's ministers, the function of the laity in ministry, and the pastoral care of the clergy. The House of Bishops has been examining the criteria and procedures for selecting the Church's ministers. Since the breakdown of the proposals for Covenanting the Synod has identified a need for an agreed theology of ministry and the priesthood. This strategy, while not pretending to solve any or all of these problems, is intended to assist their resolution by building on what has already been achieved and by providing the stimulus to debate which can come from one person's vision.

THE PARTNERS-IN-MISSION CONSULTATION

4.   The vision to which I have been led is controversial. In the summer of 1981 I took part in the Partners in Mission Consultation. This was an exercise in which Christians from other traditions and from other Anglican provinces were invited to help members of the Church of England formulate its priorities for mission for the next few years. The Consultation highlighted the need for a much greater emphasis on 'shared ministry' so that the energies and gifts of the laity, too often stifled or discouraged by clerical domination, could be released for both the planning and the practice of ministry. The Standing Committee of the General Synod, in considering how best to follow up the PIM Report, asked ACCM to make 'shared ministry' an important dimension of the forthcoming strategy document.[2]

SHARED MINISTRY: A STRATEGY FOR WHAT?

5.   The idea of 'shared ministry', however, is capable of either a conservative or a radical interpretation. On the one hand it can be seen as the means by which the traditional structures, with all their proven worth, can still be

4

maintained when the number of full-time diocesan clergy has been greatly reduced (15,488 in 1961: 10,789 in 1982). With the help of the laity, and the more professional assistance of accredited lay ministers and non-stipendiary priests, the depleted ranks of the stipendiary clergy can continue to provide adequate pastoral cover and meet the general expectations of the people at large. This is not an unattractive strategy. It is also viable, because the Church of England, not least through the efforts of Archbishop Coggan, has in recent years had more candidates coming forward for ordination than most other Churches in Western Europe. If present trends continue, the decline in the number of full-time priests could level out by the late 1980s and could return to something like its present level in ten years' time.[3] But if we return to 1963 and measure our resources of full-time ministry against what was available then, and even more significantly, against what Leslie Paul thought would be necessary, the contrast is startling.

THE ACHIEVEMENTS OF DYNAMIC CONSERVATISM

6.  The cost of such a traditional strategy must therefore be calculated in terms of the strain already apparent in many of the parochial clergy and their families, lost opportunities for ministry outside the parochial structures, plus the assumptions about 'maintenance' which lie behind it. In carrying on its nationwide ministry during the past twenty years the Church of England has displayed remarkable life and vigour. It has shown determination to 'keep in business' whatever the cost, in the most depressing circumstances of urban redevelopment or of rural depopulation. The conservative approach to 'shared ministry' sees the ministry of the laity as the call-up of the Church's last reserves. At best the result will be 'business as usual'; at worse, for all the intense effort, the spiral of decline may continue. In the opinion of one recent author:

> 'The Church, because of its dynamic conservatism, has become satisfied with presiding over its own elaborate and time-consuming funeral service.'[4]

When one compares the situation today with the goal that Leslie Paul was setting before us twenty years ago, one must at least consider that the Church, if it goes on refusing to face the possibility of more radical change, may be in danger of losing its proper vocation.

PREPARING FOR RADICAL CHANGE

7.  There is an alternative understanding of 'shared ministry'. In its bare essentials it means that basic Christian communities should accept their vocation to be the Church and become responsible for their own ministry; at the same time the stipendiary ministers of the Church should be placed according to the priorities of mission. This is the strategy advocated here. It is not a change which could be achieved overnight. Nor, in view of the undoubted life and vigour of the Church, does it need to be. I have assumed from the discussions which have led to the request for a strategy that what is

needed is a long-term objective which might be reached forty rather than twenty years from now. An emergency operation is not in view. In characteristic fashion, the Church has already managed within its existing structures to permit the development of several variations and experiments which, if successful, can prepare the way and even provide models for a very different future. Up to now it has summoned enough energy to postpone the need for radical change in its ministry, but not enough to make such change ultimately unnecessary.

STRUCTURE AND SYNOPSIS OF THE REPORT

8.   Since 'strategic' thinking has its home in military circles, I have borrowed for this report the recommended structure of an operation order, for which the headings 'situation', 'mission', 'execution', 'administration' and 'communication' would be used. The material is here arranged in a similar way, but with mostly different headings.

9.   I begin with an analysis of the *situation*, covering both the context for ministry in a changing society and developments within the Church's ministry since 1963. Special studies are provided of the present state both of rural and of urban ministry, since it is in these areas that the consequences of the Church's reduced resources have been most apparent, and also that rapid social change has produced the most obvious problems.

10.   There follows a statement of the strategy's *aim*. It relates this to the ends which, according to current policy documents, the Church's ministry should serve. The strategy is offered as a means to achieving those ends, not a diversion from them. As an appendix to this, there is a chapter clarifying the use of such overworked terms as ministry, mission, maintenance, and community.

11.   Next comes *the strategy* itself (the 'execution'). This is in two parts. First there is an exploration of the ministry of the whole people of God, in the world and in the Church, and an identification of a number of objectives. One of these is the recognition that all Church members are called to ministry and the renewal of their baptism commitment. Another is to challenge local church councils and leadership groups to identify, with the help of consultants, their own particular needs and resources for ministry. A third is to see the provision of the ministry as the combination of local responsibility and partnership with others in sharing resources. The ordained ministry provides a means of linking the local church with the wider Church in this partnership.

12.   The second part of the strategy is concerned with particular kinds of ministry. It affirms that the Bishop is the authoriser and focus of ministry. He will lead a 'task force' of priests and deacons, some stipendiary, others in

6

secular employment, who will foster the Church's mission and provide resources which are lacking in local churches. They will normally be organised in teams and always related to cells or groups of lay people. Many of these diocesan priests and deacons will have to be seconded to local churches which are not yet strong enough to provide their own ministry, but they will not become entangled in the snares of a benefice! Deacons will replace the trained and licensed ministry of present deaconesses, accredited lay ministers, Church Army officers and social workers. In the local churches leadership teams will be identified to exercise the oversight of Christian congregations on behalf of the Bishop. They will be voluntary (i.e. non-stipendiary) and may include local priests and deacons, where the particular ministerial authorisation of the Bishop is necessary (as e.g. for sacramental ministry). For the rest, the local church will decide what forms of ministry are appropriate in its own situation for prayer, teaching, evangelism and pastoral care.

13.     The next part is concerned with *implications* of the strategy. By this is meant, not its bureaucratic organisation, but its consequences for the recruitment, training and deployment of the various kinds of ministry which are required.

14.     The final section on *the way forward* ('communication') considers first the reasons for preferring this strategy to possible alternatives, and then how these proposals might begin to be implemented.


NOTES TO INTRODUCTION

[1] *The Church's Ministry—A Survey, November 1980: A Report by the Ministry Co-ordinating Group*, GS 459, p.5, para.2.
[2] See *To a Rebellious House? Report of the Church of England's Partners in Mission Consultation, 1981*, p.31, para.110; *The National Partners in Mission Consultation: Follow-up Report by the Standing Committee*, GS 547, 1982, p.4, para.10.
[3] See the table of projections in Appendix 2.
[4] M. Paget-Wilkes, *Poverty, Revolution and the Church*, Paternoster, 1981, p.101.

# SITUATION

# 1. The Dynamics of Contemporary Social Change

15.    'The church always belongs *within the context of the world*, whether it likes it or not. Even if the clergy and the laity are only concerned with themselves and their own internal problems in the church, the world still has its word to say. If some people don't notice this, it is only because they represent the world's interests themselves, in pious guise. The church is sure to be most misused politically at the very moment when it wants to be totally "non-political". This means that it is quite simply essential for the church, every minister and every congregation to see themselves as far as possible in context, and to become involved, with all their minds and capacities, in the conditions, powers and potentialities of the society they are living in. But the context is not *the text*, and we must never allow it to become so. The church's context is society. But its text is the Gospel of Jesus Christ.'[1]

16.    These words serve as a reminder that a strategy for the future development of the Church's ministry will be seriously inadequate if it is not related to the social context within which the Gospel actually engages with people's lives. This context affects the Church's communication of the Gospel in various ways. First it does so because the Word of God is concerned with the structures of society as well as the quality of individual lives. Secondly, any attempt to communicate the Word of God, whether to individuals or to society as a whole, will of necessity assume some cultural form. Then again, an established Church such as the Church of England is inescapably part of the nation's cultural heritage and thus plays a role in providing an element of social cohesion. Speaking generally, people in this country do not so much feel that they belong to the Church as that the Church belongs to them—they 'claim the rites of passage as rights of citizenship'.[2] I have myself come across an instance of a young Hindu mother presenting her baby to the vicar for christening because she gathered from the advice of neighbours that it was part of the necessary procedure of the welfare state, like registering the birth or attending the health clinic! She had particularly kindly neighbours, because there is also the attitude that 'C. of E.' is the national religion, part of what distinguishes the true 'Britisher' from undesirable aliens. Of course it is no longer true that social convention demands that all babies should be 'done', but here again changed attitudes to religion are only part of changes which are happening in society as a whole, and these in turn have profound consequences for the Church. Some of these changes must therefore be summarised.

17. 'In the last few decades the Western world has experienced a transformation in the assumptions and habitual practices which form the cultural bedrock of the daily lives of ordinary people.'[3]

In her recent study of contemporary cultural change in Britain, Bernice Martin goes on to describe the effects of the 'counter-culture' of the late sixties in the destruction of traditional boundaries, structures and taboos. She notes the internal contradictions of this assault; it can now be seen as having been the nemesis of the Romantic movement. As a result Britain is presently at a time of significant cultural change: the 'counter-culture' has led nowhere, but having happened, there can be no return to the old order. In considering this assessment of the cultural scene it is interesting to reflect that we have entered a period of equal uncertainty in the economic field. A movement which dates from much the same time as the origins of Romanticism has similarly come to a halt, namely, the industrial revolution. Britain is becoming a post-Romantic, post-industrial society. Some like to talk of modern electronics technology as a second industrial revolution. Others describe the new era as post-industrial in the sense that economic growth and prosperity are no longer to be sustained by the concentration and organisation of labour which in the past has led to the formation of what is now an overwhelmingly urban society in Britain.

18. A third element of social change may be suggested as a philosophical parallel to the cultural and economic upheavals. In his book *The Making of Post-Christian Britain*, Dr A. D. Gilbert has described how a process of secularisation has historically accompanied industrialisation, and this has led to the pluralistic society with which we are learning to become familiar.[4] Post-Romantic, post-industrial, post-Christian: it is much easier to describe Britain in terms of what it has left behind than in terms of what it is going to be in the future. So how can we plan an appropriate ministry for the Church to exercise over the next forty years? For it must be remembered, as the report from the Ministry Co-ordinating Group in 1980 pointed out, 'that the working life of young men and women currently training for the full-time ministry of the Church will extend well into the third decade of the next century'.[5] It is useless to engage in any attempt at amateur crystal-ball gazing. All that can be done here is to look at the three critical situations of change just indicated and ask what in each case are the *dynamics of change*, what are the forces at work which are likely to contribute to the emergence of the (at present indistinct) twenty-first century Britain.

## A POST-INDUSTRIAL SOCIETY

19. 'Whereas the industrial revolution greatly increased our muscle power, the new electronics technologies have greatly extended our brain power, or capacity for information and knowledge. Just as coal was the driving force for industrialisation, information is the motive force for post industrial society.'[6]

A number of important things follow from this observation; for example, that control of information will be as crucial as control of the means of production has been. Information is not simply a neutral tool. It matters very greatly what information one is given and in what form. The consequences in technologically complex areas where society needs to take corporate decisions are enormous, as for example in the forming of public opinion over the future development in this country of sources of nuclear energy. Vital decisions affecting the environment, the quality of life and military defence are in fact increasingly being made without real public accountability or parliamentary control. The form in which information is given is the art of communication. It is important to know who will own and control cable television when it arrives. Technologically it is possible to develop community broadcasting, although opposition to this from the establishment is as predictable as were government attempts to control the pulpit and exclude 'mechanick preachers' in the seventeenth century. Trivialisation and illusion are obvious dangers of the new information technology: flexibility and freedom are among the benefits bestowed.

20. There is, however, one threat which overshadows the whole subject of increasing computerisation. It is the extent to which people are made obsolete by high technology. 60% of all 16-year old school leavers in EEC countries have no formal qualifications at all. They are obviously put at risk by the disappearance of many unskilled jobs. But the computers also execute many skilled functions as well. Ralf Dahrendorf, Director of the London School of Economics, has reminded us of the need to distinguish between work, in the traditional sense of paid employment, and activity.[7] There is of course plenty of work waiting to be done; the alternative to a job need not be idleness. Unfortunately our sense of dignity and worth is related to the recognition and remuneration we receive for work done. The problem is compounded by the traditional work ethic. In his book *Bias to the Poor*, David Sheppard advocates the development in its place of a 'life ethic', emphasising the components of a creative and rewarding life-style.[8] Despite the present lack of realism among politicians and the conservatism of the trade unions, continuing high unemployment is a force for great social change. The welfare state will need to be reconceived. Co-operation will have to replace rivalry in industrial relations. At the same time developing technology will permit new styles of work with flexibility of hours, greater equality of men and women, and greater movement between jobs with widespread implications for training and re-training.

A PERMISSIVE SOCIETY

21. The term 'permissive society' in popular parlance has a strongly sexual connotation. It can also, however, be taken as the most comprehensive brief description of what the anti-structural symbolism in the arts and the political 'Underground' of the 1960s was after. The part played by the mass media in

promoting the permissive society is obviously of significance. A small radical elite was able to influence popular attitudes beyond anything which had previously been possible. There are signs that television is now losing its non-stop audience and a possible reason for this is the spread of video equipment which gives much greater choice in the matter of what people can watch, and when. Voices are raised in concern over the lack of control in this area, but it is also true to say that there will be much more self-control or self-determination; the image-makers will no longer have the confidence that they are instantaneously influencing a whole relatively captive audience.

22. A permissive attitude to structures has spread into all areas of life. In education, for example, open-plan classrooms, the elimination of subject boundaries, and individual liberty for pupils in decisions about their curriculum have received strong advocacy. The case of education illustrates how the limits to permissiveness have become apparent leading to a return to utilitarian values. In fact the boundaries are now firmly back in place in most areas and conservatism has become the prevailing mood, with the exception that there is still great freedom in what people choose to do with their leisure, and how they behave in their private lives.

23. 'Instead of becoming a truly all-pervasive life-style the culture of expressive disorder has retreated to become a leisure time relaxation. Even there it sits alongside the equally powerful symbols of conservation and continuity in twentieth-century folk culture.'[9]

Leisure, however, is an area of the greatest significance, not only because there is more of it about than there used to be, but also because those in all social classes who have prospered from the affluent society, and thus approximated most closely to the life-style of the advertising media, have undergone a process which may be described as privatisation. The world of home, family, friends, holidays and recreation forms the centre, and life is dedicated to achieving and maintaining a desired standard of living in these areas. Pubs are improved to reach an acceptable standard as alternative homes. Churches are carpeted and provided with lounges, coffee-bars and meeting areas as alternative pubs! (The churches follow the social trends, and we need to be aware of this.) Within this agreeable, informal, warm, comfortable world the individual feels he is entitled to live out his own private life, doing his own thing without interference from the State or anyone else.

A PLURALISTIC SOCIETY

24. Permissiveness over life-styles is clearly related to a pluralism of values. Britain has not become a pluralistic society because of post-war immigration of people from other cultures, nor because of the adoption of permissive standards of behaviour. Both of these things have been built on to an existing foundation of secularism. It has been demonstrated that secularism in Britain remains profoundly influenced by Christian values. But the Church as an organisation has become marginal; a leisure-time pursuit for those who

are interested. That is to say that it is no longer at the centre of power, and social constraints no longer induce people to attend. At least, that fact has to be assimilated alongside the parallel one that the Church of England remains a venerable social institution which continues to be acknowledged by the State as in some sense guardian of the nation's morals and a vehicle for the ritual expression of national aspirations and achievements. Moreover, although toleration of personal belief is widespread in England a pluralistic outlook has by no means completely prevailed. It is unwise for 'imported religions' to adopt too high a profile, especially if they appear to have implications beyond the area of private belief. On the other hand, there is great interest in learning about foreign cultures and this has certainly been promoted by an increase in travel.

25. Pluralism of behaviour is evident beyond the strictly religious realm. Patterns of family life are becoming much more diverse; the nuclear family now stands alongside the single-parent family, the re-constituted family (children of previous marriages together with children from the new partnership), the extended family, and households of single people living together. People are weaker on institutions (the effects of the counter-culture are still evident in this private sphere) but still want the quality of relationships which the family in its various forms is supposed to provide. Nevertheless the increasing complexity of the concept of the family is something which the Church by and large has so far failed to appreciate.

26. The acceptance of pluralism also has far-reaching political consequences. It becomes difficult to achieve a sufficient body of opinion for clear policies. The result in Britain has been a developing tendency for the country to be governed by Whitehall, and there is at present no sign of this changing. Bureaucratic institutions have flourished with a life of their own rather than reflecting a corporate consensus of public opinion which does not exist. Meanwhile the boundaries of the State itself have become less certain. The EEC is gradually becoming more powerful, with potential implications for the Church of England as a national Church related to existing boundaries. Equally, the removal of power recently taken away from local authorities could lead to a backlash in the revival of the unresolved issue of the devolution of government.

27. What, in the future, can hold society in this country together? It is impossible now to return to a concept of a total Christian society in the sense advocated by T. S. Eliot a few decades ago. But neither is humanistic idealism likely to provide sufficient cement in circumstances of tension when so little social cohesion is evident. War would be unacceptable as a means to internal unity: it would be a counterfeit Armageddon. There is, on the other hand, a realism in Christian eschatology which makes it possible to see society theologically as a whole, and this is part of what the Church must be saying in its witness to the people of Britain at this time of uncertainty.

28.   There are signs that man at the end of the twentieth century is becoming increasingly aware of the narrow boundaries to his place of security, and the limits upon his ability to create his own destiny. On the other hand his capacity for self-destruction is all too apparent. These circumstances may lead to a drastic reversal of secularising trends. A quest for spiritual meaning, and for renewed contact with our inner nature, which has of course never ceased, may once again occupy much more of our attention, not just as individuals but as a society unable to reach the city of God. This does not mean automatic renewal of the historic Churches; they may prove to be empty shells, unable to house a new movement of the Spirit.

29.   In concluding this brief survey of social change the only immediate statement I would wish to make about the prospects for future ministry is that the post-industrial, permissive and pluralistic context within which the Church has to operate is neither simply good, bad nor indifferent as a sphere for Christian ministry. It remains the 'world', i.e. society organised apart from God; it remains, too, the door of opportunity for the Gospel, i.e. the world which is the object of God's love, creation and saving activity. The tensions we have noted in society are contained and dealt with creatively in the Gospel.

### i) Work and Activity

In the Fall man lost his God-given working environment, but the Gospel offers him redemption for renewed creative activity with God.

### ii) Structure and Freedom

The cultural tension between order and permissiveness is resolved in the relationship between law and liberty in the Gospel, where they both emanate from the grace of God.

### iii) Pluralism and Cohesion

Universal redemption is seen as the purpose for which God calls out a chosen people, so that humanity may recognise not in the Church but in Christ the Way, the Truth and the Life.

NOTES TO CHAPTER 1: THE DYNAMICS OF CONTEMPORARY SOCIAL CHANGE

[1] J. Moltmann, 'The Ministry of the Whole Church to the World', in *Christian*, vol.6 no.5, Epiphany 1982, p.8.
[2] B. Martin, *A Sociology of Contemporary Cultural Change*, Basil Blackwell, 1981, p.193.
[3] B. Martin, *op.cit.*, p.1.
[4] A. D. Gilbert, *The Making of Post-Christian Britain*, Longman, 1980.
[5] GS 459, p.43, para.108.
[6] R. Brown, 'Information Technology and the Christian', in *Crucible*, Jan.–Mar. 1983, p.4.
[7] R. Dahrendorf, *On Britain*, BBC, 1982, p.183.
[8] D. Sheppard, *Bias to the Poor*, Hodder and Stoughton, 1983, p.122.
[9] B. Martin, *op.cit.*, p.245.

## 2: Developments in Ministry since the Paul Report

30.  Faced with the Church's loss of membership, the attrition of its power and influence, and a worsening ratio of clergy to population, Leslie Paul chose to describe the situation for the Church's ministry as movement 'towards a critical point' rather than the arrival of a crisis, the process of reduction being a slow one. This indicates immediately why the Church is still, twenty years later, relying chiefly on its traditional strategy for its ministry to the nation. There have been difficult times before: the desperate shortage of competent clergy in the sixteenth century, the upheavals of the seventeenth century, the neglect of the eighteenth century, and the population changes of the nineteenth century all placed severe strains upon the parochial system, but it survived them all. Who can say when the critical point of breakdown is reached, or whether it ever will be reached? Compared to the situation today one wonders what the problem was in 1963. Leslie Paul's work was based on an existing ministry of full-time diocesan clergy totalling 15,488 in 1961, and the knowledge that for several years previously the annual rate of ordinations (in excess of 600) had been greater than the annual losses through death and retirement. He expected this level to increase to about 830 ordinations in 1971, by which time he anticipated that there would be nearly 19,000 clergy available. In fact we find ourselves in 1983 with fewer than 10,800 diocesan clergy and an annual rate of ordinations to stipendiary ministry not much above 300. Every year since 1965 ordinations, even with the inclusion of non-stipendiary candidates, have been well below annual losses. The parochial clergy line has become very stretched indeed.

31.  Although Leslie Paul used the best available information, the other major statistical prediction on which he based his strategy also proved to be dramatically incorrect:

> 'All the evidence goes to show that population and house building will continue to "explode" in coming decades.'[1]

As we now know, the ink was hardly dry on his paper before the birth-rate began to plummet. It is a cause for relief that my own proposals are not ones which involve statistical planning! However, in spite of events falsifying his projections, it is important to return to Leslie Paul's strategy because, as is evident from what has just been noted, it was not a response to a crisis in manpower as such, but rather a serious attempt to accept the implications of the Church of England's mission to the whole nation. There were two principal grounds for concern:

i) 'The Church . . . is likely to continue to see the ratio of parsons to population move against it.'[2]

ii) 'The inevitable effect of the parochial system of deployment is at present to place most of the parsons in the country while most of the population lives in the towns.'[3]

32.  The broad strategy which Leslie Paul proposed for a more effective deployment of the clergy was the abolition of patronage, an open system of appointments, and a limited leasehold to replace the clergy freehold. Junior clergy would accept direction during their first five years in orders. The parochial system would gradually be transformed by the creation of new forms of ministry, beginning in areas where it was most obviously failing, i.e. isolated rural areas, decaying inner suburbs and rapidly developing fringes of great conurbations. Leslie Paul estimated that perhaps one-third of existing parishes came into one of these categories. He proposed the creation of major parishes with team ministries including specialists. Other specialists would work in officially designated 'extraparochial places'. Rural deaneries would be asked to investigate forms of inter-parochial co-operation. Despite the good recruitment prospects for the ordained ministry, Leslie Paul wanted more–as many as 1,365 ordinations per annum, in addition to the development of lay ministry (including a target of 10,000 readers) and a non-stipendiary priesthood:

'I propose . . . an increase of the total ordained ministry by one-third to be deployed in the areas of greatest urban density. Only some such effort on the part of the whole Church could conceivably make a dent in the vast urban indifference with which the Church is faced.'[4]

IN THE STEPS OF LESLIE PAUL

33.  The Paul Report led to the setting up of a Commission on the Deployment and Payment of the Clergy, under the chairmanship of Canon Fenton Morley. Its report *Partners in Ministry* (CA1640) was published in June 1967. It made some influential recommendations concerning the payment of the clergy, and an important suggestion that all accredited lay ministry should be brought together with ordained ministry as part of the responsibility of Diocesan Ministry Commissions. At a national level progress in this direction was achieved in 1972 when CACTM, reorganised as ACCM in 1966, was united with the Council for Women's Ministry in the Church (CWMC). Readers' work was incorporated more slowly, both at national and at diocesan level, but a Readers' Committee of ACCM and representation of readers on the Council were established in 1977.

34.  The *Partners in Ministry* report went further than Leslie Paul in some respects in its proposals for altering the parochial system. It recommended that the diocese should be taken as the basic unit, and that the clergy should minister through being either 'on the strength' or 'on the books' of the diocesan establishment:

'The new responsibility which the Church will undertake is to ensure that a clergyman has both the opportunity of exercising his ministry in response to his own sense of vocation and in the best interests of the Church, and the means to support himself and his family while doing so . . .The Church's responsibility will extend to all clergy on the strength of a diocese.'[5]

The clergyman's terms of employment and tenure of his post were thus to be related to diocesan staffing, and private patronage and benefices would disappear. However, the legal and geographical definition of separate parishes would continue to be necessary in view of the legal right of parishioners to the ministrations of the Church of England. Two subsequent developments were to move the Church's ministry fractionally in the direction of these recommendations, but at the present time patronage and freehold rights remain basically intact (apart from the important change under the Ecclesiastical Offices (Age Limit) Measure of 1975 that incumbents who have been instituted since 1976 may be required to retire at 70). First, the Pastoral Measure of 1968 facilitated the suspension of presentation to a benefice pending a scheme of pastoral re-organisation, and also clarified the formal establishment of team and group ministries. Second, when the General Synod was instituted in 1970 it set up a Terms of Ministry Committee which led to a Clergy Deployment Working Group to assist the House of Bishops in 'the formulation of a scheme for the fairer distribution of clergy manpower'.[6] This took seriously the concern of Leslie Paul that 'most of the parsons (serve) in the country while most of the population lives in the towns'; but now, in the context of seriously declining clergy numbers, it was proposed to relate redeployment to the *Partners in Ministry* concept of a staffing establishment for each diocese.

THE 'SHEFFIELD FORMULA'

35.  The Clergy Deployment Working Group, under the chairmanship of the Rt Revd Gordon Fallows, Bishop of Sheffield, recommended in 1974 a formula, based on a number of factors of which population was the most important, to be used as a guide in calculating each diocese's equitable share of the available manpower. Each diocesan Bishop was asked 'to agree to work so as to bring the total number of his clergy progressively nearer to that allocation of the total number of clergymen expected to be available in 1980 and successive years'.[7] This way of proceeding received the endorsement of the General Synod, and proposals relating to the sharing out of each year's supply of deacons followed in 1976, together with firm diocesan targets for the number of clergy in 1981. It was envisaged that revised allocation figures would be produced from time to time as and when population changes for each diocese became apparent.

36.  The 'Sheffield formula' is thus a system of securing fair shares of clergy manpower in the dioceses. Its effect is, however, limited by the fact that it is being applied at a time when the total number of clergy is diminishing. Since

19

it is related to differences of population between dioceses it would mean that if the total number of clergy available were in fact constant or increasing then the formula would be a means of achieving the objectives of the Paul Report in furthering the Church's mission by providing extra resources in urban areas. In a time of declining manpower, however, the Sheffield quota places great strain upon the predominantly rural dioceses, which was not all the price which Leslie Paul had in mind in his strategy. He did not favour the *transfer* of clergy to the towns, but a concentration of *extra* manpower according to population requirements. The circumstances of decline which have obtained since the Sheffield quota system was brought into operation have inevitably made it into an instrument for depriving the rural areas of clergy, although this was not its purpose. This is serious in a situation where churchgoing has declined more sharply in the country than in the towns. (See Appendix 1.)

37.   The consequence has been the uniting and grouping together of several parishes under one incumbent. Pastoral re-organisation has made more effective use of what staffing remains available. The development of group ministries has stretched resources further in some cases. What used to be called 'light duty' posts have either ceased to exist, or have been combined with diocesan jobs. But there comes a point (Leslie Paul's 'critical point') at which the maintenance of a full-time nationwide pastoral ministry available to all through the traditional parochial system proves incapable of being sustained.

A TARGET FOR ORDINATIONS

38.   By the mid-1970s it was becoming clear that the future of the Church's ministry was in considerable doubt. The number recommended by the Bishops' Selectors to train for ordination to stipendiary ministry fell from 348 in 1975 to 254 in 1976. Predictions were made that 'a serious crisis in staffing is to be expected within the next decade'. Returns from the dioceses in response to an enquiry indicated that a minimum number of 11,600 full-time clergy would be needed in 1986 if the parochial structure were to be maintained in a viable form. The dioceses were further asked what they regarded as being the likely consequences if the numbers available were to fall markedly below this minimum figure. In reply some dioceses, especially rural ones, foresaw the end of the existing pattern of parochial ministry. Others would expect to stretch resources further yet by the creation of larger parishes. Others would cut back on the number of clergy in specialist ministries. Others were thinking of covering the vacant posts by recruiting non-stipendiary clergy, or by creating a purely local ordained ministry to provide local leadership.

39.   In July 1978 the General Synod received a Report (*The Future of the Ministry*, GS 374) from the House of Bishops based on this research and,

responding to the initiative of Archbishop Coggan, endorsed the Bishops' proposal that a target should be set of 400/450 recommendations annually to the 'full-time ordained ministry', as being required to maintain a nationwide parochial ministry. The implications of setting such a target for the recruitment work and training budget of the Synod were neither then nor later fully explored in debate, although the mood at the time was one of determination to do what was necessary. Some response was discernible in subsequent years. Recommendations for training for stipendiary ordained ministry went as follows:

| | | |
|---|---|---|
| 1977 | – | 349 |
| 1978 | – | 376 |
| 1979 | – | 375 |
| 1980 | – | 404 |
| 1981 | – | 361 |
| 1982 | – | 350 |

40. Numbers in training for stipendiary ordained ministry increased from 708 in October 1978 to 806 in October 1982. Numbers actually ordained as stipendiary deacons remained static between 301 and 313 from 1977 to 1982, but a rise to about 340 is expected for 1983. The target range of 400/450 recommendations has thus been achieved in only one year and there is at present no sign that it will be reached consistently. The overall picture since Leslie Paul presented his material has therefore changed as follows: the population of the provinces of Canterbury and York has increased by about four million, whereas the number of full-time clergy has declined from 15,488 in 1961 to 10,789 in 1982. The table given in Appendix 2 demonstrates how the total is likely to change over the next ten years, if certain predictions about numbers entering the ministry, and losses through death and retirement, are fulfilled. There is clearly little possibility that the minimum of 11,600 full-time priests will become available to staff the parochial system.

STATISTICS OF DECLINE (AND PARTIAL RECOVERY)

41. In terms of church membership, what Leslie Paul described in 1963 as statistics of decline now appear as comparatively impressive. Yet it is also apparent that, following a trough in the mid-1970s, the Church is showing modest signs of recovery:

| | *1960* | *1976* | *1980* |
|---|---|---|---|
| Total Baptisms | 423,000 | 245,000 | 272,000 |
| Total Confirmations | 190,713 | 94,318 | 97,620 |
| Easter Communicants | 2,339,000 | 1,681,000 | 1,764,000 |
| Christmas Communicants | 2,074,000 | 1,695,000 | 1,804,000 |
| Electoral Rolls | 2,900,000 | 1,755,000* | 1,824,000 |

(*1978 figure)

It is particularly interesting that such growth as there has been during the past few years has taken place at precisely the time when numbers of parochial clergy have become dangerously low. Is the Church therefore less dependent upon its clergy than it thinks it is? What inferences may be drawn about their pastoral effectiveness? What has happened to the basic formula used by Leslie Paul of 25 Christmas communicants per living of 1,000 and over, plus *ninety* for every full-time worker, plus ten for each additional 1,000 of population?[8] Or could the redistribution of clergy according to the Sheffield quota system have had this effect already? I think that most people who have been at all closely in touch with ministry in the Church of England over the last twenty years would have little doubt about the real reason for recent Church growth at a time of clergy decline: it has been a period during which the clergy have become *a much smaller part of the Church's total ministry*. The Church's need of the gifts of the laity has been emphasised in numerous ways: by the liturgical movement, by the charismatic movement, by the advent of synodical government, and of course by the very disappearance of the clergy.

42.    This last factor can have one of two opposite effects, as those with experience of a vacancy in a benefice know well. Either the life of the parish hangs in a state of suspended animation, or the laity accept responsibility. The former state normally operates where people have the idea that ministry of the Gospel is the function of a separate clerical caste. It is in this respect that the development of a non-stipendiary priesthood may be making its most significant contribution, just because it combines a clear call to ministry with a life-style which is also appropriate for the laity. But NSMs have to be seen as just one of a number of developments in ministry during this period, including the admission of women as readers in 1969; the growth of lay eldership schemes; the training of lay pastoral assistants; a marked growth in the number of women entering the ministry as deaconesses and parish workers; and more recently exploration of the possibilities of a local priesthood. The *Future of the Ministry* report from the Bishops in 1978 (GS 374) not only called for more stipendiary clergy, it also welcomed 'the opportunities for more effective pastoral care and for mission offered by the development of a variety of ministries, ordained and lay, stipendiary and voluntary'. It called upon every diocese to consider 'its responsibility for recruiting, training and developing the forms of ministry which the Church will need in the next 25 years'. A number of dioceses are now in process of identifying them and developing appropriate strategies. Reference will be made here to some of these forms of ministry before some conclusions are drawn from this survey.

THE NON-STIPENDIARY PRIESTHOOD

43.    The emergence of a non-stipendiary priesthood in the Church of England has not been simply an emergency response to the declining

numbers of stipendiary clergy. The Paul Report noted the existence of an unpublished report by a working party of CACTM produced in 1961. Leslie Paul revealed that:

'The report proposed an increase of the priesthood by acceptance of volunteers from other professions—not as a makeshift arrangement to tide us over man-power shortage but rather as a new dimension of the priesthood altogether which will make the work of the Church more effective among the professions and in workplaces and bring a new priestly order to the rescue of the old.'[9]

Bishop F. R. Barry, contributing to a symposium entitled *Part Time Priests?* published in 1960, had written:

'The proposal sounds revolutionary in England only because here people have been accustomed for so long to think of vicars and curates that they cannot imagine priests of any other kind. A "proper" parson is a whole-time parson . . . But then . . . Christianity is a whole-time vocation . . . What I am suggesting is a priesthood . . . which would be exercised and fulfilled partly, or mainly, in "secular" employments, partly in supplementing the whole-time Ministry.'[10]

44.     The CACTM report of 1961 urged that the time had come for active experiment. The chairman of the working party which wrote it was Bishop John Robinson of Woolwich, in whose diocese of Southwark an experiment was at that time being established of training men for ordination by means of a part-time course undertaken while continuing in secular employment. Such courses were essential for any development of non-stipendiary ministry, and as numbers of NSMs grew during the 1970s so a nationwide network of courses came into existence. Patterns of training varied to meet geographical and other constraints.

45.     A guiding principle in the recognition of non-stipendiary ministry has been that the Order of Priests is one, even though it may have varieties of expression. NSM candidates were required by the Bishops' Regulations of 1970 to attend national selection conferences and to meet the demands of the General Ordination Examination appropriate to their age group. (NSM candidates are not normally sponsored under thirty years of age.) Comparability in standards of training has been insisted on, and all part-time courses are now given recognition on the basis that they may train men either for stipendiary or for non-stipendiary ministry.

46.     In 1977 W. H. Saumarez Smith produced a survey of progress with NSM, which he chose to refer to as 'honorary ministry'. His report showed that '*quantitatively* the Honorary Ministry is no solution to the problem of shortage of ordained manpower in the parishes'.[11] By that year numbers recommended by the Selectors had increased to 109, or nearly a quarter of all ordination candidates. Since then the annual figure has been remarkably stable, being again 109 in 1982, with a peak of 126 in 1978. The uneven distribution of NSMs, and the fact that they are recruited mainly from among the professions, especially teachers, has placed further limitations on

their potential as a support for the parochial ministry everywhere. The alternative title of Auxiliary Pastoral Ministers, used in the 1970 Regulations, has now fallen largely out of use. Some dioceses, wishing to emphasise the contribution of NSMs in a sphere where the parochial clergy have little access, namely in their places of secular employment, have begun to describe these ministers as 'priest-workers'.

47. In 1982 ACCM appointed Dr Mark Hodge to undertake a full-time research project on the development of non-stipendiary ordained ministry. His report is being made available at the same time as this document.[12] It reveals that in 1982 there were about 770 NSMs in active ministry. A number of these are attempting to fulfil a ministry at work, but it is possible to predict that up to half of those selected for non-stipendiary ministry under 57 years of age will in due course transfer to stipendiary ministry. An evaluation of the present contribution of NSMs, and suggestions for their part in a future strategy, will be made in Chapter 13 below.

SPECIALIST MINISTRIES

48. There also exist opportunities for full-time stipendiary ministry outside the parochial system. Some of these (e.g. service, prison, hospital and educational chaplaincies) are outside the diocesan structure as well, and the Church may have very little say over how many such posts require the services of its clergy. At present about 2,000 priests are engaged in this category of ministry. They may be regarded as 'absent from the parochial ministry' and therefore, on present manpower levels, guilty of making a significant difference to its viability. But this would be a deplorably negative attitude. A great many of these specialists occupy positions of enormous potential for Christian ministry. Moreover, it is a significant feature that several of these areas are witnessing the establishment of new posts. For example, there were 89 full-time hospital chaplains in 1962, and this number had increased to 177 Anglican chaplains in 1982. Present plans are for up to 100 further posts in the next few years. Welcome though this is, the consequences for diocesan staffing need to be weighed.

49. The contribution which some of these specialists also make to parochial ministry either directly through spare-time help (e.g. from school and college chaplains at major festivals), or indirectly (e.g. through good liaison work by hospital chaplains), is certainly valuable. It would nevertheless be desirable to have greater co-ordination with diocesan staffing. For example, a college of technology in the London area recently decided to advertise a full-time post combining lecturing with chaplaincy work. This position was open to applicants from any denomination, but in the event an Anglican incumbent from the West Country was appointed. The diocese in which the college is situated was not consulted, nor could such consultation have been demanded. However, the new chaplain was not in a position to buy a house which could

accommodate his family close to London. His valuable but rather isolated ministry would have acquired greater significance if he could have been included in a diocesan ministry team and had access to a housing loan during his tenure of the appointment. Another unfortunate feature of the present scope of specialist ministries outside the Church structure is that so seldom is the appointment of an accredited woman minister considered. Of course part of the reason for this is the reluctance, not of the appointing institutions, but of the Church to authorise women to undertake a full sacramental ministry.

50.   Within each diocesan establishment there are specialist posts and these also have been increasing in number. Full-time Anglican industrial chaplains have increased from 28 in 1962 to 92 in 1982. In response to the enquiry in 1978 some dioceses were adamant that they would not reverse this trend in order to salvage the situation in the parishes. In one diocese, for example, during the five-year period 1973–8, the number of full-time parochial clergy dropped from 366 to 319, a decline of 12.8%. During the same period the number of full-time extra-parochial clergy in the diocese (excluding bishops, archdeacons, and cathedral staff) rose from 6 to 13, an increase of 116%; while the number of clergy dividing their time between a small parochial responsibility and a specialist appointment rose from 5 to 17, an increase of 240%. It could be argued, of course, that the numbers involved here are too small to make a substantial difference to the parochial situation, although across the country the increasing numbers of industrial chaplains, youth chaplains, social responsibility advisers, education specialists, training officers, ecumenical officers, press officers, and so on add up to a significant number of clergy. It could be asked (as it was by the contributor of an article in the *Church Times* on 22nd October 1982 entitled 'Ministry of all the talents'), why priests are necessary for these specialist posts? The answer is often because a house can be made available by combining the post with a small parish. Parochial ministry is then in danger of becoming a necessary adjunct to the specialist occupation. In fairness, however, it should be added that many of these jobs depend upon the confidence of the clergy and therefore require some experience of parochial ministry.

51.   Diocesan specialist posts may be divided into those which are expressly concerned with mission, and those which have an advisory role and seek to supply resources to parishes. There are no doubt dimensions of both types of ministry in most jobs, but the emphasis is usually clear. The existence of the second category not only contributes to, but ultimately also depends upon the continuation of vigorous and healthy parish congregations.

DEACONESSES AND LICENSED LAY WORKERS

52.   At the beginning of 1983 there were 229 stipendiary deaconesses and 104 stipendiary lay workers in parochial or diocesan ministry. In addition

there were, in November 1982, 91 Church Army captains and 38 sisters working in and largely paid by the dioceses. This gives a total of 462 full-time lay workers. When Leslie Paul referred to the contribution of stipendiary lay ministry he quoted the important fact that 'a full-time lay worker in a parish counted for as much in pastoral influence as a full-time clergyman'.[13] One would assume, therefore, that a glimmer of hope for parochial ministry is to be found in the recent increase in lay candidates coming forward for full-time work. Excluding Church Army recruits, there were a total of twenty-six candidates recommended for training in 1973. By 1981 this had risen to 116, of whom 73 were offering for stipendiary ministry. Astonishingly, voices were raised asking if there were too many candidates, and whether posts could possibly be found for all those accepted for training. In October 1982 the House of Bishops agreed that:

> 'In order to promote an effective deployment of stipendiary deaconesses and accredited lay workers, each diocese be asked to adopt a minimum establishment figure for such ministers in the years 1983 and 1984.'

At the same time the Bishops put the procedure for the placing of deaconesses and lay workers in their first posts on the same basis as that operating for deacons. Meanwhile the General Synod was moving towards the admission of women to the diaconate, including the existing ministry of deaconesses.

OTHER LAY MINISTERS

53.   Attention has been given to the development of 'accredited' forms of voluntary lay ministry in a number of other ways in addition to that of non-stipendiary deaconesses and parish workers. While the number of licensed readers has not greatly increased (6,581 in 1962; 6,759 in 1982), standards of selection and training have undoubtedly risen. Two dioceses (St Edmundsbury and Ipswich, and Ely) and a number of individual parishes have introduced schemes for lay elders. Part-time training courses have been developed which prepare men and women together for ordained and lay ministry. Some dioceses provide training for particular forms of lay ministry (e.g. pastoral assistants in Southwark). The diocese of Winchester has recently commissioned eighteen men and women to go out and train 'thousands' of lay pastors in the parishes. Some parishes have training programmes to establish a lay ministry of e.g. baptism or marriage preparation, or home visiting. Stewardship schemes have trained considerable numbers of lay people to give some articulation to their Christian commitment. The work of the RSCM and other bodies has improved the standards of the ministry of music in worship. Some parishes support full-time youth or community workers, or directors of music, dance or drama.

SOME CONCLUSIONS

54.   From this rapid survey of ministry in the Church of England during the

last twenty years I wish to draw four general conclusions which will affect future strategy:

(1) *The parochial clergy are now working under increasing pressure.* I believe that the consequences are becoming apparent in recent concern over the pastoral care of the clergy, in the incidence of clergy marriage breakdown, and in their general level of health. It is not surprising, in view of what has happened (or failed to happen) since 1963. At that time, and under those much more favourable conditions of parochial ministry, Leslie Paul was aware of the need for a ministry to the clergy themselves, and of their frequent experience of loneliness, isolation and frustration. Nothing in this report is intended to devalue the contribution of the parochial clergy. It is only because of their commitment and perseverance that the system continues to operate at all. They remain a considerable body which, whatever the strategy for the future, will continue to provide the Church's main pastoral and teaching resource. My conviction is that unless there is a massive reinforcement of their ranks (and it is difficult to see where that is likely to come from) they will continue to burn themselves out in ways which fail to liberate their ministry in the most effective manner. Even those most dedicated to shared ministry find within the present system that it is that much more exhausting and time-consuming to involve others than to carry on alone.

(2) *The vitality of the laity is evident.* The Holy Spirit is at work, renewing the Church, whatever difficulties there may be with the structures. This applies to any age, but the experience of the last twenty years in the Church of England amounts to what may be described as *the emergence of the laity.* This raises questions, as well as hopes. What is the real sphere of lay ministry? Some would say 'in the world', not 'in the Church'. Leslie Paul was aware of the dangers:

> 'The laity can become a clericalised laity, shut off from the world by habits of thought and social usage almost as completely as the ordained ministry is.'[14]

Others today would not want to make this distinction, but see clergy and laity together in the Church enabling it to be the Body of Christ fully involved in the world. The activities of the laity also raise questions about what we understand by professionalism in ministry. Most fundamental of all, however, is an acceptance of where responsibility for the Church's mission properly belongs.

(3) *There are increasing opportunities for specialist ministry.* As noted earlier in this chapter, a thoroughly professional ministry by the Church is not only still wanted, but is increasingly wanted in many institutions in this country. In addition to this the Church has begun to realise the advantages to its own life of allowing its ministers, ordained and lay, to develop their particular gifts. Nevertheless a resulting division between parochial and specialist clergy is not helpful in the development of a coherent strategy, especially when many of the latter hold posts outside the diocesan establishments.

(4) *The diocese has increased in significance as the basic unit for the deployment of stipendiary ministry.* This was desired by the *Partners in Ministry* Report and has been promoted by the working of Sheffield, which has left each diocese to decide how its allocation of stipendiary clergy should be used. In most dioceses the proportion of specialist posts has increased. Diocesan pastoral committees have been set up to decide how best to deploy the available ministers. The significance given to the diocese accords with the position of the Bishop in the Church of England as the pastor who ordains and sends out ministers and provides for the welfare of the flock. Nevertheless, whatever may be desirable in theory and expected in practice, the ability of the diocese to carry out its plans for deployment remains severely limited by the continuation of private patronage and the parson's freehold.

55.   Before developing a strategy which takes account of this situation it will be useful to look in greater depth at both rural and urban ministry, since these have been regarded as particular pressure points in previous reports.[15]

NOTES TO CHAPTER 2: DEVELOPMENTS IN MINISTRY SINCE THE PAUL REPORT

[1]L. Paul, *The Deployment and Payment of the Clergy*, CIO, 1964, p.137.
[2]*Ibid.*, p.22.
[3]*Ibid.*, p.23.
[4]*Ibid.*, p.164.
[5]*Partners in Ministry:* The Report of the Commission on the Deployment and Payment of the Clergy, CA1640, 1967, p.22.
[6]*First Report of the Terms of Ministry Committee*, June 1972, GS 87, p.30.
[7]*The Deployment of the Clergy:* The Report of the House of Bishops' Working Group. GS 205, p.15, para.39.
[8]*Op.cit.*, p.139.
[9]*Op.cit.*, p.155.
[10]*Part Time Priests?*, ed. R. Denniston, Skeffington, 1960, p.14f.
[11]W. H. Saumarez Smith, *An Honorary Ministry*, ACCM Occasional Paper no.8, June 1977, p.39.
[12]*Non-Stipendiary Ministry in the Church of England*, GS Misc. 583A, 1983.
[13]*Op.cit.*, p.150f.
[14]*Op.cit.*, p.150.
[15]E.g. *The Report of the Lambeth Conference 1978*, CIO, pp.83ff.

# 3: Rural Ministry

56.   An article by a country clergyman recently appeared in the Church press. It was intended to present an optimistic and cheerful view of the rural parson's lot. Nevertheless it ended on a note of rather dubious encouragement to those brethren who are susceptible to fits of depression: 'Until either the logic of finance forces its conclusion upon these tiny communities or, better, revival brings new life, the downward spiral of decreasing effectiveness and credibility will continue.'[1] This comment reflects a general attitude that things can only get worse in the countryside. Village schools, shops and post offices are closing; public services, especially transport, are being progressively withdrawn; chapels are disappearing and Free Church ministers are now seldom resident in rural areas.[2] The Church of England, because of its commitment to a nationwide parochial ministry, maintains a presence of a kind. But this is a mere shadow of what it used to be within the living memory of many country people. In many places it may amount to no more than a monthly service and a share in a priest who lives some miles away and is responsible for pastoral care in up to a dozen villages. The small congregation has to cope with two enormous financial burdens: one is the maintenance of this ministry, including the high working expenses entailed in visiting a scattered flock, and the other is the upkeep of a large and expensive ancient building. It is easy to doubt how much longer it will be possible to keep things going. It is easy to become preoccupied with the limited nature of the resources rather than with the opportunities for mission.

WHO LIVES IN THE COUNTRY?

57.   One point which must be given full weight is that the majority of people living in the country today have chosen to do so, and generally this will be because they prefer country life to town life. There are, of course, the rural poor who are trapped in sub-standard housing and lack some of the community services which are often available in towns (although this may be compensated for by better voluntary aid and neighbourly care). There are also those who have grown old in the country, and those who still work in agriculture and its ancillary services. These are a declining proportion of the rural population. The number of people employed in the agricultural industry is now smaller than the British Leyland workforce. There are now fewer farm workers than farmers. Yet there is no shortage of people wanting to live in the country, and the price of housing is no longer significantly cheaper than in nearby towns.  Cottages are bought by folk retiring from the towns.

The resulting high percentage of elderly people in some villages can become a distinct social problem, especially in hard weather. Many villages also have modern housing developments to accommodate people who choose to live in the country and commute to work in urban areas.

58.    The relative size of these different elements in the rural population will do much to determine the different characteristics which exist between one village and another. It is wrong to generalise about life in an English village today, since many types of rural community exist. There is also a strong inter-flow between the urban and rural populations which means that in pastoral terms it is important not to think of the countryman as a species totally distinct from the town-dweller. But if we survey the rural scene as a whole it is clear that there are large numbers of people who, in spite of the disadvantages and the financial sacrifices involved, prefer to make their home in the countryside.

## THE ATTRACTIONS OF THE COUNTRYSIDE

59.    Even rising fuel costs have not so far checked the desire of commuters and retired people to forsake the towns. What are they looking for in the countryside? Sociologists have discerned two main attractions: a discovery of identity by living in a small community, and a search for authenticity in an increasingly plastic society (advertising consistently preaches that 'natural goodness' is to be found in the countryside). With these are associated a desire for 'peace and quiet', to 'get away from it all' and to find room to breathe. Where migrating town-dwellers settle in the country in sufficient numbers some of the rundown of rural services is reversed (e.g. primary schooling) and in any case the commuter who possesses a car does not suffer too much from some of the other deprivations (e.g. poor shopping facilities).

## THE MYTH OF THE VILLAGE

60.    In order to achieve the benefits of a sense of identity and authenticity the migrant from the town must believe that traditional village life still exists. To heighten this impression ancient customs and pastimes and rural crafts are revived. Respect for tradition is one of the strengths of country folk which the Church has to work with as being itself a very powerful part of that tradition. But the cultivation of tradition as the essence of the rural way of life ignores the fact that the village's inhabitants are not economically, socially and culturally interdependent any longer. Late twentieth-century villages have a different economic base. Change may not be prevented in the country any more successfully than in the towns. The newcomers from the towns are themselves the disruptive influence they wish to escape from and they betray this by resisting further development once they have themselves taken up residence in the country. It may look as though their arrival has prevented cottages from falling down and even whole villages from becoming

deserted. This is true. But the new countryman has not saved the old way of life: he has created a new one. This, however, he is reluctant to accept.

61. In the country the Church frequently has a relationship to the community as a whole which it only very occasionally acquires in the towns. To take an extreme example, an East Midlands village with a population of thirty-four and a church set out in the fields has a monthly service attended by an average of sixteen people. As a percentage of the population this far exceeds anything achieved in town parishes. Despite increasing difficulties, it is felt in this village that the church, as the only gathering place, must be kept going because of the part it plays in keeping the community together. For this reason it is irrelevant that there is another village complete with church within sight one mile down the road. It is considered equally vital that the vicar should visit all the villagers and not just the churchgoers.

62. By and large the Church responds warmly to this feeling of being needed in rural areas in order to build up the community. What could be nearer to its true purpose? But Trevor Dorey, in a study of *Rural Ministries* carried out for the Oxford Institute for Church and Society, has warned of the dangers:

> 'With the disappearance of so many traditional symbols and landmarks, the church often becomes the sole focus of village identity. Church membership is then seen by some largely as a commitment to the village itself, as identification with the local community, rather than as a conscious participation in a believing and worshipping group. The results can be an inclination to assume proprietary rights while denying anything more than nominal obligations, and it can lead on occasions to the virtual imprisonment of the Church by the village.'[3]

63. Of course the clergy who work in the countryside must be people who are interested in village life as a whole, and are able to work with the religious expectations of the community, but there is a need for the Church to witness in rural society both to the catholicity of the Church and to the interdependence which exists in the modern world between one local community and another. The element of escapism and withdrawal on the part of those who remain economically dependent on the towns must be challenged. Each village, however small, is of course a unit of pastoral care and this must be taken into account in a strategy for ministry. But if the shortage of clergy today makes it necessary to link most villages up in a wider network of ministry this can be turned to advantage in helping to break down the myth of the self-contained community. Few tears should be shed over the disappearance of the late Victorian country parson, ministering for perhaps forty years or more in possession of the freehold of a single benefice. His ghost could not be comfortable in a modern-sized vicarage surrounded by executive homes and mechanised farming.

64. The rest of this chapter will be concerned with exploring further the possibilities of these wider networks of ministry, but first there must be some consideration of the unquestionable change that has occurred in what has traditionally been the greatest strength of the parochial system in the Church of England, namely, the availability of individual pastoral care. From the standpoint of the pastors themselves, the country clergy generally feel that they succeed in keeping in touch with their parishioners when they are divided between two or even three villages. Beyond that there is a sense of diminishing effectiveness to the point where credibility is in danger of being lost with responsibility for perhaps six or more villages. This is a generalisation. But from the standpoint of the parishioners there is a change not simply in the amount but in the nature of the pastoral care being offered as soon as there is no longer a resident incumbent. To quote Trevor Dorey again:

> 'There is a need for an alternative door to knock on in times of crisis and for alternative eyes and ears in each place. Real community, after all, can only be fostered by local residents.'[4]

But this is continually happening quite naturally. There is no need in a country parish to organise a sophisticated visiting scheme and an elaborate structure of street wardens. Village neighbours are inevitably aware of each other's needs. It is a question therefore of identifying those 'natural pastors' who are able to share the incumbent's aims and work with him rather than seeing him as one on whom to make demands. One particular home may become the priest's base when he is in the parish and the 'focal point' of pastoral care when he is not. Once training in shared ministry has developed the gifts of the laity contacts made through this 'focal point' need not invariably be referred to the incumbent.

## SHARED MINISTRY IN THE COUNTRY

65. It is unlikely that many smaller villages will have sufficient resources for the local Church to undertake a fully shared ministry without the support of clergy and readers drawn from elsewhere. This is not to deny the vocation of every baptised Church member. A handful of committed Christians may well feel that they lack some of the more particular gifts of leadership, teaching and pastoral care. In any case they also need the stimulus and vision that is denied to the unit which operates on its own without hearing what the Spirit is saying to the churches. The image of the Body of Christ from 1 Corinthians 12, with its different members each having a part to play, is usually applied to the local Church as a single congregation. In the country it is important to relate it to a wider field of interdependence. Most reports which have been prepared on the question of developing a local ordained ministry have stressed the vital importance of doing this only within the context and as part of a fully shared ministry involving both stipendiary clergy and the laity. Few villages could at present produce ministerial teams

of this kind on their own. So a future strategy, while providing for 'focal points' in each village, must cease to think in terms of individual parish units for deployment of ministerial resources.

THE LOCAL CHURCH IN THE COUNTRY

66. The local Church in the countryside, apart from some exceptional cases, is not best seen as confined to a single village. It is true that it can be difficult to discern the existence of one body when the inhabitants of the next village are regarded as foreigners. And the true configuration of the local Church will not necessarily correspond to the number of parishes which have to be put together under the care of one incumbent. The emergence of rural group ministries which began at South Ormsby thirty years ago suggested another way of looking at the local Church. This pattern has not developed in quite the way which might have been expected. But it has prepared the ground for a different kind of group ministry in villages where only one full-time priest is now available: for what we are now beginning to call a shared ministry. The leadership of the local Church in areas of the countryside is undertaken by teams including at least one stipendiary priest, and a number of non-stipendiary ministers, ordained and lay, who have been put forward by the congregations in the locality acting together. There is a wide variation in the ways in which this approach can be developed to suit local requirements. A number have been imaginatively described by Canon Christopher Newton in his paper, *Life and Death in the Country Church* (BMU, 1981).

THE TRULY RURAL DEANERY

67. Once we argue that the rural ministry of the Church should be more co-ordinated than is possible with individual parochial units it becomes necessary to consider the place of the deanery. Christopher Newton, who is a Rural Dean and country parish priest in the Oxford diocese in addition to his work as Bishop's Ecumenical Officer, sees the deanery as more than a means of communication between parish and diocese. It has also the functions of enabling the Church to collaborate with other institutions, and of co-ordinating the resources and activities of the Church's mission. In the countryside there are special opportunities of supporting the parishes through training courses, information and publicity, exchanges of ministers and team visits. Dr Anthony Russell has expressed a more limited view of the really rural deanery. He regards it as 'an artificial construct within the Church designed principally to facilitate easy communication'; he would question the wisdom, particularly in rural areas, of giving it more significance than this:

'To adopt the deanery as the basic pastoral unit of the churches involves a significant change in our understanding of the nature of the church. No longer would the church be a "community church" for such a change would transform it into an "associational church" and would have the effect of further distancing the church from the life of the local community.'[5]

68.  The conclusion we would wish to draw here is that each rural parish, as a distinct community, must remain a basic unit of pastoral care, but that ministerial resources, development and planning should be grouped to cover wider areas in which the local Church operates a shared ministry, and the deanery offers possibilities of development for this purpose.

## CAN THE RURAL DEANERY BE THE LOCAL CHURCH?

69.  It is unlikely that this group ministry can often be coexistensive with a deanery as we have deaneries at present. The local Church must be something which remains related to a particular locality with common roots deeper than those of modern ecclesiastical or civil planning. There are, however, a few deanery group ministries, for example at Buckingham and at Pontesbury in the north of Hereford diocese. One advantage of a deanery group is that the laity then have a constitutional place in decision-making which is not always safeguarded in joint planning between deanery and parish level. The requirements of synodical government are, however, doubtfully compatible with the extreme variation in size which would result if the deanery were made to correspond to the truly local Church in all country areas.

## RURAL ECUMENICAL PROJECTS

70.  In the countryside it is often argued that ecumenical relationships are less important because other denominations scarcely exist. In fact the smallness and slender resources of the rural parish make the scandals of disunity even more apparent. Weakness is not an argument for unity, but neither is the absence of chapels and Free Church ministers and Roman priests an argument for disunity. Non-Anglican Christians will be found in most villages. What is needed is a new concept of local ecumenical project, not based on ordained ministers of different denominations working together, but on Christians of all denominations being encouraged to act together as the leaven of the Gospel in their local communities, with the support of their respective church authorities.

## THE CHALLENGE OF RURAL MINISTRY

71.  As one case study puts it: 'If large rural areas are not to be unchurched, there must be adventure in ministry.'[6] Adventure, however, is not the easiest of concepts in many rural communities where conservative instincts predominate, often particularly among newcomers. Those stipendiary clergy who continue to be deployed in the countryside face the hardest challenge of all. They themselves often come from the towns and have the difficulty of understanding the attitudes of country folk. But whether the people are prepared to contemplate change or not the clergy must learn to come to terms with a new role because the traditional pattern of parochial

ministry has already disappeared over large tracts of the countryside. The country parson is no longer part of the rural hierarchy as in the nineteenth century. Nor can he continue to be an elderly priest who has taken a lighter cure in the latter years of his ministry, as in the earlier part of the twentieth century. Encouragement can be taken from the fact that in the past, despite appearances, radical changes have taken place in rural ministry. At times this has come about through strife which has left its mark for generations in places where memories are long. But change has also been wrought by patience, love and the winning of trust.

NOTES TO CHAPTER 3: RURAL MINISTRY

[1] Article by P. Skoulding, *Church of England Newspaper*, 23 July 1982.
[2] E.g: 'Facilities and services in rural Cambridgeshire are clearly in decline...The rate has clearly accelerated in the late 1970s and early 1980s.' (*Cambridgeshire Villages: A Guide to Local Facilities*, published by Cambridgeshire Community Council, 1983, p.4f.)
[3] T. Dorey, *Rural Ministries*, Oxford Institute for Church and Society, 1979, p.8.
[4] *Ibid.*, p.24.
[5] A. Russell, 'What about the really rural deanery?', *Church Times*, 23 April 1982.
[6] *Tap Roots No.10: Rural Norfolk—Loddon and the Raveningham Group*, BCC, 1980.

# 4: Urban Ministry

SOCIAL SEGREGATION IN THE CITY

72.    'Urban ministry' is a term which can be applied to a wide variety of the Church's work. Much of this ministry can, and more of it certainly should, be a response to opportunities for mission in the city which occur outside the structure of the parochial system. But even in geographical terms it is important not to forget that both the suburban and the inner-city parish are part of the same urban enterprise. This is more evident in the smaller manufacturing and market towns, but the great conurbations include not only the city centres, the inner-city redevelopment projects, the council housing estates and the respectable middle-class suburbs, but also many mixed areas where shops, factories, schools, hospitals and a wide variety of housing all co-exist in a kind of string of urban villages. The underlying unity of city life must not be lost sight of by the Church, and indeed an important part of its ministry to the city will be to give expression to this unity. Nevertheless it is obvious that social forces are at work which constantly tend to divide the 'haves' and the 'have-nots' in the towns.

73.    Bishop David Sheppard has described this process in his book *Bias to the Poor*:

> 'The dominant philosophy in countries like Britain and the United States is that you will naturally want to "make it", to go up in the world to give your children a better chance of success. The effect of such a philosophy on the community from which you come is compounded by housing policies which segregate owner-occupiers from council tenants in huge one-class quarters. The bigger the city, the more this process has taken place, with the assumption that those who are successful will always choose to move away from the communities in which they grew up. This has happened for generations–it inevitably tends towards creating communities of the left behind.'[1]

WHAT ARE URBAN PRIORITY AREAS?

74.    The concern of this chapter is with what are coming to be known as 'urban priority areas' to indicate places where deprivation and social need are most obvious and concentrated as a result of the process just described. It will be argued that such areas need to be given priority in a strategy for the Church's ministry, but first it is necessary to give clearer definition to the areas in question. A recent report entitled *Churches in Urban Priority Areas* from the diocese of Liverpool used the residential categories distinguished by Merseyside County Council's Planning Department, which are as follows:

1a. Areas of established high status
1b. Areas of modern high status owner-occupied development
2. Rooming house areas with concentrations of single young persons and privately rented furnished accommodation
3. Inner/deprived council estates of very low status
4. Outer council estates
5. Areas of older terraced housing with much privately rented unfurnished accommodation
6. Retirement areas.

In the Liverpool report's analysis categories 2–5, containing 64% of the population of Merseyside, include all the 'urban priority areas'. That does not of course mean that almost two-thirds of the population of Liverpool live in such areas, but it is in the residential categories so defined that deprivation and poverty of various kinds exist. Similar, if not identical, categories would apply elsewhere.

WHO ARE THE POOR?

75. Deprivation and poverty are relative terms. Who, after all, are the poor? It has been cogently argued that the poor are not a separate class of people, but poverty is a condition to which the entire working class is at risk at certain points in the life-cycle, particularly during child-rearing, old age, unemployment and ill health. This situation has been modified by the provision of social benefits, although there continues to be the notorious 'poverty trap' of the welfare state. At the same time, housing re-development policies have taken away one most important resource against poverty which existed in traditional communities of residence, namely, the natural neighbourliness of extended families living close together and of friendships continuously cemented in pubs, streets, corner shops and back-to-back housing between people who often also worked together close by. It is not altogether fair to blame the disappearance of these networks of support entirely on the planners, because smaller families, working women, and the spread of car ownership have also tended in the same direction.[2]

76. This analysis apparently continues to hold good in a time of economic recession and continuing high rate of unemployment when the tentacles of poverty are spreading out towards an increasing number of people. There is of course a sliding scale of deprivation. But long-term unemployment creates a new attitude, which was expressed to me by one elderly man who can remember the depression between the wars: he is quite clear that the difference now is that many seem to be giving up hope that things will get better. In these circumstances there is emerging what may almost be called a non-working class. There are parts of our major cities where unemployment is as high as 50%. In particular, the inner-city areas and inner council estates are becoming inhabited by losers in the urban race: black and coloured

people, single-parent families, non-coping families, students, ex-students and drop-outs, the old and the vulnerable.[3]

77.   It is precisely in these 'urban priority areas' that the Church of England appears to be often weakest in its membership and finding it hardest to sustain its mission. Why should this be so? The alienation of the industrial working-class from the Church has received a great deal of attention, and it needs qualification in various ways. If the working man has not in the past embraced Christianity he has nevertheless suffered it a good deal. Until recent times a high proportion of children in northern industrial towns went to Sunday School. Many families were recipients of the charitable resources administered by the Church. Bishop Mervyn Stockwood, reflecting on his ministry in down-town Bristol before the war, says that 'the main difference between a parson in such an area in the 1930s and one in the 1980s is that a parishioner can now tell him to go to hell!' He is glad that society's casualties are no longer dependent upon 'Lady Bountifuls in clerical collars'.[4] In addition to the identification of the Church as representative of the privileged classes the impact of the Protestant work ethic needs to be measured. David Sheppard recalls how 'the membership of a relatively strong inner-city congregation was described to me as "good working class", with the emphasis on *good*. The great majority would be in employment.'[5] Bishop Stockwood could remember hearing a sermon in which someone else who later became a Bishop said that he had never known a converted Christian who had been unable to find employment. It is not surprising if the unemployed have concluded that the Church of England is not for the likes of them.

CAN AN INDIGENOUS CHURCH TAKE ROOT IN URBAN PRIORITY AREAS?

78.   As the existence of deprivation spreads in the cities the 'urban priority area' (UPA) parishes find themselves struggling in what frequently appears to be a losing battle for survival. The Liverpool report describes the ways in which the financial odds are stacked against the poorer parish:

> 'Many of the UPA parishes have low parish incomes and live with constant financial anxiety. Where many live on social security the margin for increasing income is low, whereas overheads (insurance for example) are often actually higher in UPA parishes. Almost everything must be paid for from income, whereas in richer parishes gifts in kind (a lectern, a set of hymn books, etc.) are more frequently made. The UPA parish is less likely to have a treasurer with the skills to handle parish accounts to the best advantage.'[6]

79.   The residual congregations of such parishes are upon examination very often found to contain a high proportion of people who have 'bettered themselves' and moved away from the locality but who still return to church –moreover they retain positions of leadership in these congregations. In Toxteth it was recognised a number of times 'that churches situated in

working class areas, which were dominated by the middle class background and aptitudes of the clergy and the aspiring, commuting, lay leadership, failed to reach their full potential and relevance to the local community'. The Liverpool report concluded:

> 'No church can be a truly local church so long as the leadership and decision-making is in the hands of people who do not live there.'[7]

80.    The people who do continue to live in the urban priority areas are, as has already been indicated, those who have had repeated experience of failure and discouragement. The resulting lack of self-confidence is something which effectively tends to suppress any qualities of leadership and responsibility which individuals may possess. 'I'd hope more than anything, that people's confidence in themselves and in God should grow against all the odds,' was one housing-estate vicar's assessment of what was needed.[8] This is clearly a priority. But is the potential there for the development of indigenous leadership? The very process which has created the community of the 'left behind' has ensured that what remains is in certain important respects an 'unnatural' community. Those who stand out, those with imagination and creative flair, those with the skills to influence others, are not likely to be left in the decaying inner-city or housing estate. Such natural leaders as do appear seldom subscribe to church membership.

81.    Against all this three things need to be borne in mind. The first is that the style of leadership to be looked for is something very different to what may be considered appropriate in a suburban parish, and all the evidence of community action indicates that a leadership which is *sui generis* is always ready to emerge in urban priority areas if sought and encouraged. Secondly, where an indigenous leadership has been called out in UPA churches difficulties have been encountered less in finding the right people than in the failure to provide adequate support for them. And thirdly, it is the conviction of clergy who work in urban priority areas that the potential is there. As one group of Manchester clergy expressed it to me: 'People remaining in the inner-city not only need God, but are capable of finding Him and also of communicating Him.'

WHY PRIORITY AREAS?

82.    It may be accepted that the position of the Church of England is weak, not to say desperate, in most urban priority areas. Such weakness, however, does not necessarily justify a decision 'to redistribute our financial resources to further the mission of the church in inner-city areas' as taken by the General Synod when it debated how to follow up the Partners-in-Mission Consultation at its November 1982 group of sessions. There is an alternative strategy to one of pouring resources into needy areas. Sir Angus Maude has summarised the issue in an article describing the current crisis in the Church of England:

'In essence the argument is about whether it is better to reinforce moderate success and hold your ground, or to attack the forces of paganism where they are strongest.'

He makes his own sympathies clear when he continues:

'Why on earth, cry the rural faithful, can you not leave the parsons with those who actually want to go to church, instead of drafting them into hopeless missions to the pagan city-dweller?'[9]

There is an extreme irony in his use of the word pagan here, stemming as it does from the Latin for a countryman and thus serving as a reminder that the strength of the Christian mission in the ancient world was in the towns, while the rural population clung to their folk religions! It is too late to play off rural ministry against urban ministry in this way. The real choice for the Church of England now is between putting much greater resources into urban priority areas and pulling out of them altogether. The latter course would represent a failure to 'stand alongside the poor' as the Gospel requires and as the PIM Report asked us to do[10] and constitute a final demonstration that the Church of England is a church for the privileged, as the poor have always suspected.

WHAT RESOURCES DOES THE URBAN CHURCH NEED?

83.   The General Synod has resolved 'to redistribute our financial resources to further the mission of the church in inner-city areas'. What does this imply? There is of course an unhelpful way in which the rich can undertake 'mission to the poor' and the legacy of this approach is still evident in British cities. Interviewing the Archbishop of Canterbury in a *Credo* programme for London Weekend Television on 18th April 1982, David Tereshchuk declared that 'the vulnerable and the inarticulate seem to us, certainly in our travels around the inner-cities over the last year, to almost resent your intrusion'. He was referring to the image of the Church of England as 'a powerful and wealthy institution'. We shall here look briefly at some of the implications of a possible 'urban aid programme' by the Church in terms of ministers, buildings and partnership.

SENT TO PREACH GOOD NEWS TO THE POOR

84.   It is essentially good strategy to reinforce points of strength, but this does not mean deserting the inner-city in favour of the suburbs. It means looking for the points of strength in the inner-city itself. One of these is undoubtedly the presence of trained clergy, deaconesses and Church Army officers. It has often been pointed out that among those who supply essential community skills in needy areas, including teachers, doctors, policemen, solicitors, health workers and social workers, it is generally the Church's ministers alone who actually live among the people they serve. Through the presence and availability of its ministers the Church 'sticks it out' in tough districts where other agencies may not persevere, or indulge merely in dressing up 'show' projects. Clergy and lay workers can thus enter into the

lives of those who feel powerless and voiceless and perhaps interpret their needs to the councillors and planners who take the vital decisions affecting their lives. The mere presence of the Church's ministers, however, while a potential source of strength is no guarantee of effectiveness. Several other factors must be taken into account.

### (1) Cultural distance

There will have been little in the cultural background or initial training of many stipendiary ministers to prepare them for work in urban priority areas. The implications for training will be considered later in this report, but what about the cultural gap? The history of Christian mission, though littered with awful mistakes, nevertheless proves that the minister of the Gospel is called to cross cultural boundaries. To do so effectively he or she must (i) respect the culture which already exists; (ii) distinguish between the Gospel and cultural expressions of it; (iii) be committed to long-term and practical involvement in a particular culture. These things are recognised in overseas missionary work—but they apply equally to ministry in multi-cultural Britain.

### (2) Serving the local Church

The stipendiary minister 'from outside' must be clear about his or her role. The objective will be the building of a strong indigenous Church, that is to say one in which local people are responsible for and confident about undertaking the mission of the Church in that place for themselves. The stipendiary minister is neither conducting a one-man mission nor installed as the Church's local manager.

> 'Staying a long time in a situation helps the professional leader to learn when it is right to respond to what he is asked to do, and when it is right to insist that local people work matters out for themselves.'[11]

Some stipendiary ministers may be maintained in urban priority areas to engage in community projects or undertake sector ministries. In Southampton city centre the pattern has been for team ministers to combine neighbourhood with other sector responsibilities.[12] In this way skills are supplied which may be lacking in the local Church. But the overall concern at all times for stipendiaries must be to build up the local Church so that it becomes itself the agent of mission.

### (3) Danger of isolation

Stipendiaries should be maintained in ministry, not merely paid. Long-term ministry in an urban priority area (though preferably not confined to one parish) will require a good support group including other colleagues in the area, local people and outside consultants. Proper rest and holidays are also essential. Some urban parishes have overcome the risk of burglary and vandalism in empty vicarages by arranging for retired or non-stipendiary clergy to live in while the parish priest and his family are on holiday. Despite the need of the Church in urban priority areas to develop strong, local leadership no-one would suggest that this could be achieved by withdrawing stipendiary ordained and lay ministers. Priority needs to be given to re-inforcing the diminished numbers of those who are committed to this ministry and to establishing a high level of morale in all urban teams and deanery chapters. The Liverpool report on *Churches in Urban Priority Areas* includes a necessary recommendation, but one which implies a serious judgment on the Church's attitude to its 'down-town' parishes:

> 'We urge the Church at large, and clergy in particular, to examine current attitudes to "career" and "status" in the ministry and to consider the possibility of vocation to areas of particular need.'[13]

Is that not an astonishing statement for a Church working party to have to make about its ministry?

### WHAT SORT OF BUILDINGS?

85.   The urban skyline still contains many 'fingers of God': church towers and steeples pointing skywards through the grime of human industrial activity or decay. These traditional church buildings are just as great a burden of maintenance on the inner city congregations as are the rural churches in deep country parishes; sometimes more so, because the buildings often lack the architectural merit and picturesque surroundings which attract external support for village churches. In their own way also the urban churches continue to be powerful symbols like those which adorn the rural landscape. Should the Church's 'urban aid programme' include money to keep large buildings standing, even when no more than a tiny handful actually use them regularly, just because they convey a message in stone? In an area where the population is fairly stable and there has not been a major housing redevelopment the building will have strong community associations in addition to its symbolic significance. People will have in their homes wedding portraits of family groups outside the church. The destruction of such buildings comes very close to an announcement of desertion by the Church. Yet it is verging on blasphemy to spend hundreds of thousands of pounds restoring an under-used church in the midst of urban deprivation. David Sheppard has described an alternative way in the example of St Matthew's, Brixton, where the building no longer belongs to the Church of England but has been handed over to a community trust, and as a result receives public funds for its maintenance as a local amenity:

> 'If that shedding of security and power and that wide community use are possible with a historic Church building, comparable schemes must be possible with other Churches and Church halls.'[14]

In a number of other instances church buildings have been converted into multi-purpose premises, and in some cases are being run in co-operation with the local authority to serve community purposes. It is important to make a diocesan consultancy service available to give advice on such schemes.

86.    Where there has been major redevelopment the case is different: a fresh approach is possible. The Church in urban priority areas appears to need three kinds of meeting-place. One is a purpose-built community centre which can be constantly staffed and where facilities are available for small and large groups to meet. Secondly there is a use for a low-profile point of contact with those in any kind of need. For this purpose a shop-front has provided an effective doorway in some places. Thirdly the small cell-group for worship and training requires no more than a front parlour in somebody's house. In fact this can appear to be like asking for the moon. A professional sociologist who grew up in a Lancashire mill town points out that everyone was clear about what the front room was for—'for show and for courting. Nowt else.'[15] However, I have taken part in enough Christian cell meetings in front parlours in Lancashire, the Midlands and North London to know that here the Church is presented with an opportunity to work through the existing culture to speak powerfully about the nature of the household of God.

87.    The other problem of buildings concerns the vicarage. In some urban parishes this can be dramatically different from any other housing around it. Many clergy naturally wish to be identified with their parishioners by living in a similar type of house. This is not always ideal from the point of view of their work, which must inevitably to some extent be done from home and entail visitors to their home. A vicarage which is an integral part of the church plant can be designed to combine the necessary privacy and public availability while at the same time giving some security from vandalism to the church. Since the vicarage is evidently part of church premises in this situation comparisons are not invited between different sizes of accommodation. Behind the vicarage door, however, there is another problem to be measured in terms of the cost and strain on the families of clergy called to minister in urban priority areas.

PARTNERSHIP IN THE GOSPEL

88.    Two quotations from David Sheppard about government policy in urban priority areas can be applied equally well to the Church as it seeks to follow-up the PIM Report:

> 'The long-term target is not to have generous welfare benefits, but sufficient resources in each community for it to develop its own strengths...There has been too much dominant leadership from outside the local community, providing people with facilities they did not ask for.'[16]

The urgent need for a truly indigenous Church, responsible for its own mission, has led a joint working party from the dioceses of Liverpool and Manchester to call for the ordination of local priests to serve in urban parishes:

> 'The fundamental case for a locally ordained ministry lies in the conviction that within the urban areas of our cities there are indigenous people, often lacking in confidence, with gifts and abilities, but who could be freed and appropriately

trained for leadership in ministry within their culture . . .They could uncover Christ in areas unreached, even unreachable by those who, however able, have their roots, their origins, their formation, within another culture.'[17]

There is no suggestion, however, in their report that stipendiary ministers should be withdrawn from urban priority areas. A strategy which replaced them with unpaid local priests while continuing to staff more affluent parishes with stipendiaries would create two classes of priesthood for two classes of parish. The 'device' of local priests would then prove to be the feeble death-throe of a Church which felt guilty about deserting the inner-city.

89.   It will be argued in this report that stipendiary ministers should continue to serve in all areas where the Church lacks particular local resources, regardless of ability to pay quotas. It is their dominant leadership role which needs to disappear, particularly where their presence tends to suppress the initiatives and insight of local people. Much the same applies to all external support; it is a difficulty in any scheme for twinning suburban with inner-city parishes. Yet the suburban Church needs to be aware of the experience of the Church in the inner-city. The whole Church needs to feel the one-ness of its mission; there is therefore an opportunity for mutual enrichment in such links. Human prickliness and paternalism will get in the way, but a fragmented Church will proclaim the Gospel imperfectly to fragmented communities. Sometimes group or deanery structures can help association to take place without an 'us-them' atmosphere developing. Partnership in the Gospel is ultimately the only way forward for the Church in the city, and it is a sad illustration of the difficulties of achieving this that so few local ecumenical projects have been established in inner-city areas. In this context it is important to consider what a local ecumenical project would look like which included black-led pentecostal and holiness Churches.[18] The most convincing expression of partnership appears when Christian individuals and families deliberately reverse the flow of those who are 'getting on' in the world and choose to live in and be part of the Church in urban priority areas.

NOTES TO CHAPTER 4: URBAN MINISTRY

[1]*Op.cit.*, p.10f.
[2]See K. Roberts, *The Working Class*, Longman, 1978, pp.66–79.
[3]See J. J. Vincent, *Into the City*, Epworth, 1982.
[4]M. Stockwood, *Chanctonbury Ring*, Hodder and Stoughton with Sheldon Press, 1982, p.28.
[5]*Op.cit.*, p.44.
[6]*Churches in Urban Priority Areas*, 1982, p.9.
[7]*Ibid.*, pp.7, 22.
[8]D. Sheppard, *op.cit.*, p.26.
[9]Sir Angus Maude, 'Crisis in the Church of England', *Illustrated London News*, April 1982.
[10]*PIM Report*, p.42, para.166.
[11]D. Sheppard, *op.cit.*, p.190.
[12]See *A Parish for a Modern City: Southampton Team Ministry, 1973-82*, June 1982.
[13]*Op.cit.*, p.25.
[14]D. Sheppard, *op.cit.*, p.104.
[15]B. Martin, *op.cit.*, p.59.
[16]D. Sheppard, *op.cit.*, pp.181, 190.
[17]*To Match the Hour*, A Report of a Working Party set up by the Bishops of Liverpool and Manchester, June 1982, p.19f.
[18]See below, Chapter 17.

# AIM

# 5: Statement of Aim of the Strategy

ARE WE PREPARED FOR CHANGE?

90.  From our survey of the present situation of the Church's ministry the increasing difficulty of maintaining it along traditional lines has become apparent. These difficulties, however, are unlikely to be sufficient in themselves to induce commitment to an alternative strategy. The response to proposals for radical change today is still likely to be similar to that which greeted the Paul Report and the *Partners in Ministry* Report in the sixties, so long as these proposals are seen as essentially a matter of re-organisation. Leslie Paul himself reflected on this in a book published in 1973:

> 'Much of the resistance of the clergy to my own report arose because I was more concerned with function than tradition and with effective organization than historical institution...The years have underlined and made more acute the anomalies and absurdities I sought to expose ten years ago . . . It is of course the traditional church structures in the Church of England and elsewhere which stand in the way of the proper development of human and material resources. These have everything to do with historical forms and the stubbornness of tradition, but very little, I am inclined to think, with Christianity.'[1]

That last remark is sufficient (perhaps calculated) to produce vigorous rejoinders from many Anglicans that tradition, especially 'the Tradition', has a very great deal to do with Christianity. It is because of this conviction, and because of a belief in the virtues of gradually developing institutions, that the Church of England is so resistant to the planners and the organisation men.

ARE THE EXISTING STRUCTURES FLEXIBLE ENOUGH?

91.  In the work just referred to Leslie Paul acknowledged that there are at least two significant ways in which the Church of England of the 1970s was displaying an ability to adapt its legal and institutional framework to meet the changing demands on ministry. First, the parochial system itself was 'not a grid of unyielding squares, but something like an irregular wire mesh which can be pulled and pushed a little this way or that'.[2] The second change has been the growth of non-stipendiary ministry, which could be regarded as a laicization of the priesthood. With these, and so many other, evidences of the resilience of the traditional structures, what is the case for radical change? Leslie Paul answered this mainly in terms of external pressures. For example, in 1969 there were 97 parishes with a population in excess of 20,000 each, making a combined total of more than 3.7 million. They were served by 339 clergymen. At the same time a further 3 million people distributed across the rural shires were ministered to by 3,000 clergymen. 'The

discrepancy is simply appalling,' commented Leslie Paul.[3] Since then, as we have noted, a scheme for the redistribution of the clergy has been introduced, although this has done nothing to solve the problem of the integration of parochial with non-parochial, 'specialist' ministries.

92. This study is not primarily about organisation. It does not concern itself with questions of deployment in any detail. It offers a strategy which relates not so much to existing external pressures upon the Church's re-sources, as to its own understanding of what it is called upon to be and to do. If there is to be radical change, it can only be acceptable if it carries with it some kind of theological imperative. The strategy is based upon two essential ideas which must be weighed and tested in debate before any commitment is made in the direction suggested in these pages. Any modification of the proposals put forward here will be compatible with the aim if it is consistent with this basis. The two ideas may be expressed as follows:

i) *The local Church, as the Body of Christ in a particular place, should be responsible for undertaking the ministry of the Gospel in its own area.*

ii) *The Bishop, as chief pastor in the diocese, should be responsible for ensuring that each local Church has, from within its own resources or from those of the diocese, the ministry which it needs.*

What is understood by the 'local Church' and what is included within the responsibility of the Bishop, will be explained in later chapters. The whole of the strategy is a commentary upon these two statements; the only comment at this point is to indicate that together they express one of the historic strengths of Anglicanism: a combination of the virtues of congregational and episcopal church order.

MEANS AND ENDS

93. A strategy is a means to an end. It is no part of my purpose to suggest changing the ends in view in respect of the Church's ministry. There is both an aim *of* ministry, which is unchanging (see the definition in the next chapter), and an aim *for* ministry, which may be gathered from current policy documents in the case of the Church of England. The most relevant of these at the present time are as follows:

*The Future of the Ministry: A Report Containing Thirteen Resolutions of the House of Bishops*, May 1978 (GS 374)

*The Church's Ministry—A Survey, November 1980: A Report by the Ministry Co-ordinating Group* (GS 459)

*The National Partners in Mission Consultation: Follow-up Report by the Standing Committee*, October 1982 (GS 547)

Reference may also be made to:

*To a Rebellious House? Report of the Church of England's Partners in Mission Consultation 1981* (referred to as *PIM Report*).

94.   From these documents *the aim of the strategy to be formulated here may be expressed as follows:*

  i) To ensure that the ministry of the Church of England is responsive to the demands of mission to the nation and not merely limited to the necessary requirements of maintenance (*PIM Report*, para.110; GS 547, paras.10, 31).

  ii) To make adequate pastoral care through the ministry of Word and Sacraments available in every place (GS 374, third resolution; GS 459, paras. 13–16, 83).

  iii) To encourage the development of a fully shared ministry by means of:

  a) an educational exercise to make all baptised members of the Church of England aware of their calling from God: and

  b) the supply of appropriate resources, help and training to enable them to use their gifts to fulfil their calling (GS 459, paras.95, 96; *PIM Report*, paras.110, 111, 151, 152; GS 547, para.10).

  iv) To develop in each local Church a concern to undertake effective ministry in the local community (GS 459, paras.106, 112; *PIM Report*, paras.151, 157, 159).

  v) To carry out the above (i–iv) in such a way as to contribute most fully to the ecumenical witness of the whole people of God (*PIM Report*, para.160).

95.   I am therefore concerned to discover the best means of achieving the agreed ends of the Church's existing policy for its ministry, as set out in the relevant documents, bearing in mind the particular constraints, resources and opportunities which are likely to exist over the next forty years. The result will have implications for future revision of policy; in fact, major revision of policy is hazardous without the development of a long-term strategy first (cf. GS 459, para.2; GS 547, para.9). But it is relevant to comment at this point on four particular policy matters because they already have in 1983 certain question marks attached to them.

*(1) Number of Stipendiary Priests*

In 1978 the General Synod endorsed the Bishops' 'recognition of the continued need for a full-time stipendiary ministry of at least the present size' (viz. 11,549 diocesan clergymen in 1978) and consequent call for the numbers recommended to train for stipendiary ordained ministry to increase to the range of 400/450 annually (GS 374, fourth and sixth resolutions). We have already noted in Chapter 2 that these targets are unlikely to be met. In consequence the future of the parochial system is in doubt, and I do not propose a continuation of the policy of attempting to staff a nationwide parochial system with the available stipendiary ministers.

## (2) The Future of the Parochial System

The report GS 374 emphasised the need 'to maintain a nationwide parochial ministry' (GS 374, third resolution). The 1980 survey of the Church's ministry, while continuing to seek a ministry available in every place and affirming 'the Church's mission to the whole community', also considered 'that the parochial system itself now requires re-assessment' (GS 459, paras.13, 88). This strategy attempts to carry out such a re-assessment, on the basis that the parochial system, however much it may taken for granted, is but one means to achieve the aim defined in (ii) above.

## (3) The Ordination of Women

While I personally expect with some confidence that women will be admitted to the Order of Priests during the period covered by this report there is but one major respect in which the strategy could be affected by the timing of the Church's decision on this matter. If women were to be ordained as priests in the very near future then the traditional policy of GS 374 would once again become a realistic option. This is the one way in which the numbers of stipendiary clergy could be rapidly increased: there are existing women ministers (333 stipendiaries in 1982) who in most cases have been fully trained to the requirements for ordinands, and in many cases are conscious of a call to ordination as priests. The number of women candidates has greatly increased in recent years, and there is good hope that future combined numbers of men and women offering for stipendiary ministry would be well up to the target range of 400/450 recommendations each year. Moreover, the cost to the Church of training and maintaining such numbers in the stipendiary ministry would be little affected, because the stipendiary women ministers *already exist*: it is simply a question of whether they are to be priests or not.[4] I do not believe that this issue is best determined by considering the factor of the shortage of stipendiary clergy alone, and even if a decision on this matter had already been taken, the strategy set out in this report would still be offered as a better way for the future. Under those circumstances, however, it would also be possible for the Church to continue depending on the familiar strengths of its full-time parochial ministry. There are many ways in which the style of ministry is affected by the sex of the minister; and the Church is surely impoverished by its failure to make full use of the potential ministry of women: nevertheless the broad strategy here advocated is one which can be pursued whatever the proportions of men and women engaged in each category of ministry.

50

## (4) Relations with other Churches

One result of the failure of the Covenanting proposals is a fresh determination to find a way by which the Churches in this country can come to accept each other's ministers. The results of this quest are still in the future and it has been impossible in writing this report to presuppose anything about the progress of Church unity over the next forty years. The strategy does not therefore take into account the existence of the officially accredited ministers of other Christian Churches, but it *does* look for the increasing co-operation of all Christian people in ministry through their local churches (see below, chapters 9 and 17).

NOTES TO CHAPTER 5: STATEMENT OF AIM OF THE STRATEGY

[1]L. Paul, *A Church by Daylight; a reappraisement of the Church of England and its future*, Macmillan, 1973, pp.165, 175.
[2]*Ibid.*, p.155.
[3]*Ibid.*, p.167.
[4]The recent Green Paper from the Church Commissioners on *The Historic Resources of the Church of England*, GS 563, 1983 uses the term 'Sheffield' Man to indicate the number of clergy allocated to dioceses under the 'Sheffield' formula, but with clergy not paid from diocesan funds (bishops and cathedral clergy) excluded and stipendiary deaconesses and licensed lay workers (including Church Army officers paid by the dioceses) added. The total available ministry in this category at the end of 1982 was 10,971 stipendiary clergy, deaconesses and lay workers. (See GS 563 Schedule 1, p.59.)

# 6: Some Working Definitions

96. The aim of the strategy already outlined contains of necessity some terms which may have variable theological and/or sociological content. Some of these (e.g. pastoral care, shared ministry, gifts, vocation and local Church) will receive some definition at appropriate points in what follows. There are four terms, however, which are of such fundamental significance and frequent use that an attempt will be made to explain the way in which they are being employed before proceeding any further. They are: ministry, mission, maintenance, and community.

MINISTRY

97. Ministry is service to individuals or to a community. In this country the tradition of public service was formerly expressed by the description of government departments as ministries, and the government itself as an administration. At its broadest, ministry is simply meeting human need of any kind. To speak of Christian ministry is not to limit the subject to the Church or to spiritual needs alone. It is a concern to meet human need with God's resources. This involves prayer, thought, speech and action to offer the Gospel in the power of the Spirit wherever people are falling short of the glory of God. But Christian ministry is needed just as much within the Church as outside it. The New Testament description of ministry concentrates on the mutual service to one another of fellow-believers by means of which the whole Body of Christ grows to maturity. Through 'every-member ministry' Christians use their particular gifts in active membership of the Body of Christ. Their common ministry is one of service to the world. Thus there is a distinction between ministry *in* the Church and the ministry *of* the Church, but there is no tension between the two in principle, because a Christian's primary vocation is always and everywhere to serve God. Both concern for one another and commitment to the world find their inspiration in the Christian assembly for worship. This totality of the Christian ministry is obscured not only by its traditionally restricted reference in the Church of England to those who are in orders, but also by the contemporary social context in which public service is 'normally paid, professional and highly organized'.[1] No such qualifications are necessary for the exercise of Christian ministry. Although the canon law of the Church of England refers to the clergy in using the term 'the ministry', it will be clear in what follows that no such restriction is intended except where it is made explicit that the reference is specifically to ordained ministry.

98.   Mission is the dynamic directive behind Christian ministry. It may be thought of as the 'act of being sent'. Ministry may be responsive; mission always implies the taking of initiative. It describes the divine initiative, sending the Spirit forth in creation, in inspiration of men 'sent from God', in incarnation of the Word when 'the Father sent the Son to be the Saviour of the world'. It describes the stirring of the Church by the Spirit to continue Christ's mission to announce the kingdom, to baptise the nations, to bring reconciliation to all mankind. Mission is in the heart of God: it is therefore the Church's true vocation. A Church caught up in mission is a Church on the move, taking fresh initiatives, exploring new beginnings. In his provocative study of the meaning of mission entitled *Christianity Rediscovered*, Vincent Donovan, Roman Catholic missionary to the Masai of Tanzania, writes: 'There is something definitely temporary about Paul's missionary stay in any one place. There is something of a deadly permanence in ours.' He goes on to spell this out:

> 'Paul built no priest house or missionary residence . . . He put up no buildings in which to instruct his catechumens. He built no church in which his new Christians could worship. In short, he neither built nor established a mission. *He* was the mission—he and his companions—a mobile mission, a temporary mission in any one place, a team in motion and movement towards the establishment, not of mission, but of an indigenous church, resulting as a response to his preaching of the gospel.'[2]

When the Church is established does the mission therefore cease? No, because the local Church then continues the mission: Vincent Donovan's telling point is about the way in which Paul refused to get entrenched in any one place, but passed on responsibility to others to continue what he had begun, giving the Gospel their own cultural expression, not his.

MAINTENANCE

99.   It is difficult for a Church like the Church of England, which has been established for centuries, to recover the freshness of mission which inspired the early Church. The Gospel has become so culturally encrusted by the place of the Church in our national heritage that for some it seems that the only way to recovery is to separate the Gospel from the institutional Church and begin again. Others do not even see any hope of beginning again because the message will not be new; Christianity has been rejected and Britain is now a post-Christian society. Whatever is meant by this term, it has been well demonstrated by sociologists of religion that established cults become pre-occupied with maintenance, and especially so in positions of relative decline. This applies not only to keeping buildings standing and services going and stipends abreast of inflation, but also to the place of the Church in society, the role of its public ministers, and even its attitude to mission. There is a 'maintenance' view of mission which sees the need for new members in order to ease the problems of maintenance. Recently there

has been a clear call for the giving of Church members to go beyond maintenance to the creation of 'budgets of opportunity'.[3]

100.   Nevertheless maintenance is not all bad. Where the Gospel takes root there are new Christians to be nurtured; where the Church grows it takes cultural form and is then able to express spiritual continuity by the maintenance of its tradition, its liturgy, its buildings. Coping with cultural change then becomes one of the most sensitive issues for the Church to face. We argue over it today as though it had never occurred before: we do not even know whether it is permissible to replace worn medieval statues on the west front of a cathedral with modern ones. The point is that cultural change is a continuous process in which the Church has always been involved, but as the Church becomes more and more marginal to society it is increasingly faced with a choice between a sectarian religious sub-culture which is 'faithful' to the tradition, or a re-interpretation which recognises the prevailingly secular values, assumptions and expectations of society at large. In practice, it goes on hoping for a middle way.

COMMUNITY

101.   Community operates at many levels. There is the national 'commonweal' which gives unity and identity to the nation. There is the family, which provides most people with their most intimate experience of community through the close ties of kinship and shared accommodation. Community is living in association with others. Today it is usual to speak of 'fragmented communities' to describe the results of a significant process of social change. This has made a distinction between 'communities of place', where people are conscious of assocation because they are neighbours, and 'communities of interest' where association comes through work, or recreation, or education together. It is really more accurate to speak of fragmented lives than fragmented communities. Each community may be complete enough in terms of its own identity: it is just that people divide their time between different communities more than was usual in the past. This is not necessarily disruptive. There is not always a greater sense of wholeness about living, working and playing with the same group of people over a long period of time, which can be restrictive as well as supportive. Communities can certainly 'break down' and fail to fulfil what is expected of them, but this does not appear to be a feature peculiar to modern communities.

102.   In speaking of the ministry of the Church to the community it is necessary to remember that the Church is itself a particular kind of community: one of interest, though not merely as a leisure-time activity; one of place, though not limited to the sanctuary; one of relationship, though not exclusive of any stranger. This essential community takes its significance from the Gospel, not from the existence of Church structures. Formal

54

recognition of 'the Church' by 'the community' (e.g. at national level) does not convey to the community, nor does rejection deprive it of, the Church's experience of living together in the Gospel.

NOTES TO CHAPTER 6: SOME WORKING DEFINITIONS

[1] K. Grayston, 'Can the New Testament still say anything to us about Ministry?', a paper given at a conference on *Ministry in the Church*, held at King Alfred's College, Winchester in April 1981.

[2] V. J. Donovan, *Christianity Rediscovered: An Epistle from the Masai*, SCM Press, 1982, pp.36, 100f.

[3] *A Responding Church: A Report on the Finances of the Church of England, 1980-1983*, prepared on behalf of the Central Board of Finance and the Church Commissioners by their Joint Liaison Committee, 1982, p.7, para.11.

# THE STRATEGY – 1
# THE MINISTRY OF THE
# WHOLE PEOPLE OF GOD

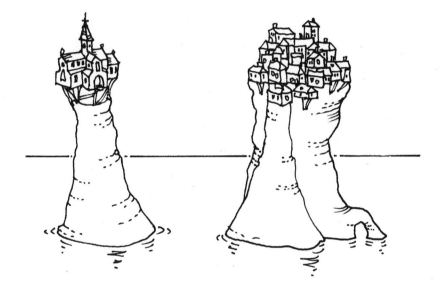

# 7: The Church in the World

103.   Sociologists of religion have distinguished between two types of Church which are variously labelled but which we will refer to as the 'communal' and 'associational' types.[1] The 'communal' Church expresses the religious experience and enshrines the religious symbols of the particular culture in which it exists. It is, in principle, the religious aspect of that culture; the distinction between membership of the Church and membership of the community is vague or non-existent. If, through a process of secularisation, the religious symbols of the community lose their force, or come to be focused elsewhere, the 'communal' Church must change radically or wither away. Conversely, so long as the traditional religious symbols retain their significance it is very difficult for the 'communal' Church to avoid identification with the conservative elements in society which are resistant to change. The 'associational' Church, on the other hand, is composed of people who subscribe to a particular set of doctrinal formulations and are prepared to meet the necessary demands of membership. There is no doubt about the resulting distinction between the Church and the community in which it is situated. This type of Church has a 'gathered' congregation made up by the voluntary association of individuals, who may or may not all live in the local community. Even if they do, their Church membership probably implies an act of dissociation from the values of the community and an accompanying sense of mission, not to change the community as such, but to persuade other individuals to transfer their interests and allegiance to the Church as an alternative community. An 'associational' Church is not one which lacks a sense of community–far from it; but it is essentially enlarged by a series of individual decisions to enter its fellowship.

A TENSION IN THE THEOLOGY OF THE CHURCH

104.   What sociologists have observed reflects a tension which exists in Christian understanding of the nature of the Church and its mission. The distinctiveness of the apostolic community is not in doubt:

> 'Jesus' life of service, his death and resurrection, are the foundation of a new community which is built up continually by the good news of the Gospel and the gifts of the sacraments. The Holy Spirit unites in a single body those who follow Jesus Christ and sends them as witnesses into the world.'[2]

There is no dispute either that membership of the Christian community is by baptism, expressed through the bestowal of a sacramental sign on those who make an individual decision to turn to Christ, or, in the case of infants where

59

they are accepted, upon the profession of faith of those responsible for their Christian nurture. The tension becomes apparent, however, when it is asked on what basis a person is qualified to undertake the Christian nurture of a child brought for baptism. The 'associational' Church would restrict this to parents who are themselves in active membership. The 'communal' Church would accept any parent or surrogate belonging to the defined community to which the Church relates, and would see Christian nurture as something shared by the community as a whole.

105.   The crucial question is whether the Christian mission is seen as involving a confrontation between two communities—The Church and the 'world'—or whether, in any given community, there is an interpenetration of Church and 'world', so that the 'world' is found in the Church and the Church is found in the 'world'. To be faithful to the Gospel the Church must declare the separation of those called out of darkness into light. As John Baker puts it in *The Foolishness of God*:

> 'It is by separation that the Church preserves—no, not her own identity! that is insignificant—but the identity of Jesus and his Gospel.'

But he goes on to refer to Jesus' description of his disciples as 'the salt of the earth':

> 'Just as there is no point in having salt unless you put it into the cooking, so there is no point in the Church's separateness unless she is also united with the world, integrally involved in it. Her separateness and her involvement are totally different in kind.'

The member of the Christian community must accept that he remains a member of the 'worldly' community. Likewise there is good reason, if contact is essential to the Christian mission, why the 'world' should be welcomed into the Church (it will find its way in anyhow!); John Baker's plea is for an 'open' Church:

> 'If the truth is to reach men through the spirit of the Christian community, then the organization and structure of that community must be adapted to establish a living continuity with them.'[3]

THE CHURCH OF ENGLAND IN THEORY AND PRACTICE

106.   If we look at the organisation and structure of the Church of England, we find that it is in theory and also constitutionally a 'communal' Church *par excellence*, with a historic involvement with the life of the nation going back to the tribal conversions of the Anglo-Saxons. The relationship of Church and State, the place of the diocesan bishop in civic affairs, the nationwide parochial system, all exhibit at different levels the character of the Church of England as the Church of the English people. In practice the picture is rather different. The progress of secularisation has made all Churches marginal to society by depriving religious symbols of their ancient power to communicate a vital understanding of human existence. Furthermore, in a pluralistic society the position of the Established Church has increasingly become one of form rather than substance: no leader of the nation could refer exclusively

to the Church of England as bearer of religious truth, and no Archbishop of Canterbury would crown a Sovereign without associating himself with other Christian bodies in the action. Finally, at parochial level, even though the Church of England may continue to behave as a 'communal' Church there are certainly few urban parishes at any rate where the Church is related to a local community in any real demographic or membership sense. People may well select a dose of religion on the same basis as they choose between brands of a product in the supermarket: the preferred 'flavour' may be C. of E. because that is what they are used to, but if another is more convenient or more attractively presented it will do instead. In working with this changed situation the Church of England has in very many places become an 'associational' Church in its attitude to *mission* (regarding it as the recruitment of individuals in competition with alternative claims to truth), while still behaving as a 'communal' Church in *membership* (by admitting the parishioners' right to baptism, marriage, burial and inclusion on the electoral roll merely on the basis of residence). The first step in a strategy for ministry must be to think more carefully about the implications of this situation.

IS THE CHURCH BECOMING A EUCHARISTIC SECT?

107.    There are many who do feel uncomfortable with a description of the Church of England as 'a religion demanding minimal commitment, and requiring neither deviation from the generally accepted ethical and social standards of the wider society nor burdensome donations of time, money or energy'.[4] For some time a movement has been at work to call the laity to much higher levels of commitment in worship, stewardship and ministry. The Parish Communion has made the Eucharist the centre of the worshipping life of many parishes with the result that regular involvement in worship has necessarily posed the questions of readiness for confirmation and preparation to receive the sacrament. Stewardship programmes have increased both the church's income and members' understanding of the need for planned giving. Lay participation in worship, expressed in ways such as lesson reading, the leading of intercessions and administration of the sacrament, has turned the liturgy into a focus of the ministry of the whole people of God. All of this has served to make the committed faithful into a clearly identified and closely knit group. They have come to regard themselves, in many parishes, as the local Christian family. The parish priest identifies with this group and sees his role as their enabler rather than attempting the apparently impossible task of being pastor to the whole community.

108.    It is possible, from this evidence, to regard the Church of England as wishing to become a thoroughly 'associational' Church. Demands are made for the ties with the State to be broken; a more rigorous discipline is wanted over acceptance of candidates for baptism. Some see a picture emerging of the Church as 'a eucharistic sect':

'The Parish Communion movement has encouraged the trend towards an enclosed conception of the local Church. Evangelism becomes an invitation to join a particular identifiable group of people, for whom the liturgy is designed.'[5]

In his article Christopher Lewis prefers a more 'open' Church: 'People should be able to drift in and out, without being embraced, given a covenant form and asked to run a club.'[6] This is a caricature, although there is an important point here about being sensitive to the different kinds of outsider. There will always be those who seek in the liturgy a vehicle for conveying a sense of mystery without wishing to let the resulting sense of one-ness with humanity compel them to make contact with the other people in church! But there is really no need for the Church of England in its present state to worry about a higher level of commitment in its *membership*. Over and over again it is clear that it is precisely the level of commitment of Church members to their faith and to each other which is attractive. Christopher Lewis gives us a much more important clue in his article when he refers to the impact of the Parish Communion movement on the Church's attitude to *mission*. He calls for: 'a parish less comprehensive in its organisation of people's lives, concentrating less on the gathered community of committed worshippers, more on the wider society.'[7] The danger comes not from having a body of Christians committed to each other in the Lord, but from the self-contained society which may result.

THE MINISTRY OF THE CHURCH IN THE WORLD

109.    The first point in the strategy must therefore be to recognise that the Church of England is called to be, and must become, a 'communal' Church in its approach to *mission*. In an interesting unpublished paper entitled 'Training for non-professionalised, non-stipendiary, lay ministry', Ruth Etchells observes that 'a high proportion of those currently training for what till now has been called "lay ministry" thought of themselves as in the future being a sort of clergy person'. She goes on to give a description of lay ministry which is worth quoting at length:

'*To be called to lay service* is to be called to live fully in the secular world, to be at ease in it, to know its idioms and its assumptions, to engage in its arguments and affairs, because one's *centre* is there. It is not to sally out from one's "real" centre, the parish church and its affairs, or the diocesan structures, for sorties into industry or trade or education or politics or whatever. It is to *live* in industry or trade or education or politics, to earn one's income from them (or to be unemployed by them); to be committed to them: and there, in that place where one's energies are committed, to engage quite consciously in mission and ministry. It is to see oneself as committed for work outside the "club" of the Church... All such lay ministers ought to be commissioned by their parishes and sent out to their task, and then supported by weekly prayer for them in the parish church, by counselling, and by a support group within the parish/deanery. But their function is not to keep the Church going as an institution, but to draw their support, comfort, sustenance and theological depth from it as they work in Christ's name in their secular calling.'

Here the priority for the ministry of the whole people of God to be engaged in mission in the world is made absolutely clear. It is equally clear that the Church has often thought of lay ministry as assistance for the clergy in running the parochial organisation. How can the commissioning of lay ministers for this 'ministry of engagement' be expressed?

BAPTISED FOR SERVICE

110.   An immediate reaction to the passage just quoted may be to object that although there may be some who have such special responsibilities for witness through their secular occupations that they must not be expected to undertake much by way of ministry within their local churches, this understanding of lay service applies in principle to the every-day witness of all ordinary Christians, rather than to the work of special ministers. That is precisely correct, and for this reason the form of commissioning which Ruth Etchells calls for must be one which is applicable to all Christians. One is provided in baptism. In the New Testament the significance of baptism includes authorisation for ministry because it includes the gifts of the Spirit (1 Corinthians 12.1–13; Ephesians 4.1–7). Every baptised Christian has been called to and authorised for Christian service in Christ's name, as a member of the body of Christ, the people of God. Baptism as currently practised in the Church of England does not make this clear; nor is it easy for it to do so in the case of infants. There is no agreement at present about the significance and timing of confirmation, and that, like baptism, is a once-for-all event. It would be wrong to institute a new form of commissioning for service unrelated to baptism.

111.   Another possibility is proposed for this strategy. Baptism as incorporation into Church membership is unrepeatable; but baptism as authorisation for ministry can be re-activated by the renewal of baptismal vows in an appropriate context. Such a context might be provided at Easter, New Year, the patronal festival, or at the renewal of the electoral roll once every six years. (A form of service is provided in *The Alternative Service Book 1980*, pp.275–8.) Whichever is chosen as most appropriate the object would be to form a 'ministry roll' of those prepared to renew their baptismal vows in this context. It would be parallel to, but not necessarily identical with, the 'electoral roll'. Inclusion on the 'ministry roll' would indicate willingness to engage in an adult training programme. Training does not authorise people for Christian ministry–that is the effect of baptism–but all who take their vocation seriously realise that training equips them to fulfil their ministry through an effective development of their gifts. The need for the Church to recognise these gifts will be examined later in Chapter 11, and more will be said about the proposal for a 'ministry roll' in Chapter 10. But before going any further with practical proposals it is important to stop and examine the basis on which lay Christians have come to be viewed as ministers and involved in what is widely referred to as 'shared ministry'.

## NOTES TO CHAPTER 7: THE CHURCH IN THE WORLD

[1]Cf. B. D. Reed, *The Dynamics of Religion: Process and Movement in Christian Churches*, DLT, 1979, pp.157ff.

[2]*Baptism, Eucharist and Ministry*, Faith and Order Paper No.111, WCC, Geneva, 1982, p.20, para.1. Hereafter referred to as *BEM*. (Also known as the Lima Text.)

[3]J. A. Baker, *The Foolishness of God*, DLT, 1970, p.336f.

[4]A. D. Gilbert, *op.cit.*, p.112.

[5]C. Lewis, 'The Idea of the Church in the Parish Communion', *Crucible*, July–Sept. 1982, p.119.

[6]*Ibid.*, p.121.

[7]*Ibid.*, p.120.

# 8: Shared Ministry

112.   The Church of England now has fewer than 11,000 full-time diocesan clergy; whereas the sect of Jehovah's Witnesses claims to have 88,000 ministers in Britain. The explanation of these apparently surprising statistics is that every active member of the Jehovah's Witnesses is reckoned to be a minister, and it is impossible to be a member without being active because the very essence of membership is to get out and about witnessing. Thus it used to be necessary for one elderly, blind lady belonging to the sect to stand out in all weathers holding *Watchtower* magazines at the gates of an Anglican theological college! While not necessarily supporting this particular approach to ministry, much Christian thinking in recent years has also been emphasising the share in ministry which belongs to every Church member. This has become a starting point for many statements about ministry, but even so it was the opinion of the Partners in Mission Consultation which took place in the Church of England in 1981 that this message has not yet been properly heard:

> 'We are still dominated by the false view that the ministry of the Church is confined to bishops, priests and deacons. The whole pilgrim people of God share in ministry, and clergy and laity must be trained for this shared ministry.'[1]

113.   Part of the problem is the idea that Christian ministry is limited to a particular area of pastoral and liturgical activity which normally belongs to the clergy. Lay participation in ministry thus becomes something of a desperate measure prompted by a diminishing supply of clergy. But as we have seen there is a much wider view of ministry. An American woman named Nell Braxton Gibson wrote an article entitled 'Is this not Ministry?' which was published in the *Audenshaw Papers* for September 1981. In it she described her involvement with her family, her friends, her community, and concluded with these words:

> 'The true meaning of ministry is service. The meaning of *laos* is people. I am a lay minister because I am one of the people who serve.'

She felt able to say this simply because she was a Christian, and not because she had any accredited or official ministry in her Church.

114.   But on this basis, what is *not* ministry? Helen Oppenheimer has referred to the manner in which, in our modern talk, ministry has become a greedy concept:

'The notion of ministry tends to gobble up everything into itself so that it becomes impossible to sort out what is not ministry. All are ministers but some are more ministers than others . . . "They also serve who only stand and wait." Who is anyone to say that someone else is not even standing and waiting? But then does it amount to much to call somebody a minister? Unless ministry can be distinguished from something else which is not ministry, it seems hardly worth talking about.'[2]

115.   It is conceivable that we could set about reversing the trend of all these modern reports, and cease speaking of all Christians as ministers. There are other words which describe the general service of God in terms of e.g. 'witness', 'discipleship', 'stewardship', with which many Christians might feel happier. But this is merely to alter terminology. Helen Oppenheimer's point is that, whatever words we use, our whole emphasis upon ministry is in danger of obscuring something of even more fundamental importance. The glory of the laity is not that in the Church we are all ministers, but that we are all members of the people of God. As Helen Oppenheimer remarks, 'To feed at God's table should be quite as awe-inspiring as to wait at it.'[3] The status of any Christian, therefore, is not in bearing the office of a priest, or a churchwarden, or an organist, but in being by God's gift a baptised member of the laity, and whatever ministerial roles are undertaken by any persons within the Church have as their object the service of the people of God.

116.   Having made this point we shall continue nevertheless to speak of shared ministry because membership of the people of God involves a call to serve one another in the Body of Christ, and together to engage in mission to the world:

'As God has called you, live up to your calling . . . There is one body and one Spirit, as there is also one hope in God's call to you; one Lord, one faith, one baptism; one God and Father of all . . . But each of us has been given his gift.' (Ephesians 4.1–7 NEB)

Baptism does therefore include an authorisation to minister as a Christian, and ministry is in fact more than a role; it is a way of being the Church, the means of expressing that care for others which is the true 'agape' at the heart of the Christian life. There is a mutual interdependence in Christian ministry because God has given us each different gifts. This is the whole point of St Paul's analogy of the human body (1 Cor. 12). The total ministry of the Body of Christ includes the response of every member to a call to share in the service which Christ himself gave to others.

THE COMPREHENSIVENESS OF THE MINISTRY OF THE LAITY

117.   In common speech 'lay' means 'non-professional', and it does so precisely because in the past the Church has been understood to be made up of, (i) the clergy as the professionals (so when the clergy teach, the Church

teaches; when a person is ordained he 'enters the Church'); and (ii) the rest who belong, but lack the skills, or the dedication, or the knowledge of the clergy. Lay status has therefore been expressed in negative terms and this is carried over into thinking about shared ministry when it is divided up into ordained ministry and lay ministry, with the latter being exercised at some less exalted level than that enjoyed by the one who occupies the altar and the pulpit. In the steady development of lay ministry which has been taking place since the middle of the last century it has gradually become recognised that those who are not ordained may have an important contribution to make to the theology, the spirituality and the liturgy of the Church. 'What is the province of the laity?' asked Mgr George Talbot, writing to Archbishop Manning in 1857. 'To hunt, to shoot, to entertain. These matters they understand, but to meddle with ecclesiastical matters, they have no right at all!'[4] By contrast the Church of England in 1866 established the Office of Reader to provide an opportunity of ministry for committed laymen. But a clear differentiation of roles between ordained and lay ministers was observed, for those admitted were not allowed to preach or to officiate in consecrated buildings, which were the preserve of the ordained ministry.

118.    By 1965, the Decree on the apostolate of the Laity from the Second Vatican Council sounded a very different note:

> 'The laity, too, share in the priestly, prophetic, and royal office of Christ and therefore have their own role to play in the mission of the whole People of God.'

Nor was this role seen as one which could only be fulfilled 'in the world', for:

> 'the laity have an active part to play in the life and activity of the Church.'[5]

In the Church of England a parallel development has brought lay ministry right into the sanctuary; indeed, readers are often regarded primarily as service-takers, and other lay people are to be found administering the sacrament and undertaking liturgical ministry in various ways. All too often the effect of developments in lay ministry has in fact been an obscuring and confusion of roles. The Partners in Mission report sums it up by saying:

> 'There is a widening of the understanding of ministry in today's Church. This we welcome, but we recognise that it is causing a crisis for both clergy and laity in their understanding of their own roles.'[6]

The crisis arises because it is considered that there must be something called lay ministry which signifies non-clerical ministry. The role of the laity is still being defined in negative terms which are not much different from those of Thomas Arnold, who described the laity as 'the Church–minus the clergy'. In fact the ministry of the laity *is* the ministry of the whole people of God. It embraces all the particular kinds of ministry, including those undertaken by Church members who are in orders, which go to make up the Church's total service of God.

119.   We have now encountered the first of two major changes in traditional
language about ministry resulting from a renewed biblical theology of the
Church which in recent years has received wider acceptance in theory than it
has found expression in practice. This is, in short, an acknowledgment that
the ministry of the laity *is* the ministry of the Church. The second, rather
startling adjustment of language comes from the realisation that the most
appropriate term to describe the whole ministry of the laity is 'priestly
service'. Lay ministry is priestly ministry! All Christian ministry is offered
first and foremost to God, so Scripture speaks of the calling of every
Christian in priestly and sacrificial terms:

> 'You are a chosen race, a royal priesthood, a dedicated nation, and a people
> claimed by God for his own, to proclaim the triumphs of him who has called
> you out of darkness into his marvellous light.' (1 Peter 2.9, NEB)

> 'Offer yourselves as a living sacrifice to God, dedicated to his service and
> pleasing to him. This is the true worship that you should offer.' (Romans 12.1,
> GNB)

> 'Through Jesus, then let us continually offer up to God the sacrifice of praise,
> that is, the tribute of lips which acknowledge his name, and never forget to
> show kindness and to share what you have with others; for such are the
> sacrifices which God approves.' (Hebrews 13.15f, NEB)

Christian social action, concern for justice, acts of compassion, building of
community are all priestly in character, not just because they are dedicated
to God, but because they witness to God's own activity. To do this they must
depend on the direction and power of the Holy Spirit and be an expression of
the life and self-offering of Christ, in whom God was reconciling the world to
himself. (2 Cor. 5.18–6.1.) As the Agreed Statement of the Anglican-
Roman Catholic International Commission (ARCIC) puts it:

> 'All Christian ministry . . . flows and takes its shape from this source and model.'[7]

Christ provides not only the example for our service of God, but the perfect
sacrifice which renders all other sacrifice obsolete. The Church can undertake a reconciling ministry in the world only if it is abiding in Christ and
living in the power of his Spirit. The ARCIC Statement goes on to say that:

> 'The goal of the ordained ministry is to serve this priesthood of all the faithful.'[8]

It is a fundamental weakness in the life of the Church today that despite a
clear statement of this kind so many of the laity continue to regard themselves as a sort of clerical support system. The function of the laity as the
Body of Christ is neither to be excluded from the sanctuary nor to take over
the role of the clergy. It is to serve God *both* in the liturgy *and* in the world.

ASPECTS OF SHARED MINISTRY

120.   'The ministry of Jesus Christ is corporately shared with the whole Church.'[9]
There are various ways in which this comprehensive view of ministry
requires a style which is increasingly referred to as *collaborative*.

## (1) Collaboration between Ministers

The very fact of the distribution of different gifts to each one should prompt ministers to work together, ordained with lay, men with women, young with old, intellectual with practical, prophetic with pastoral. This sharing is not limited to formal teams of ministers; it is the partnership which results from accepting each other as truly called into an 'every-member' ministry. There is a shared source of ministry in Christ, and a shared task, but there are different gifts and different roles.

## (2) Collaboration in Leadership

One particular role is that of leadership. There will be opportunities later to look both at the leadership required from the Bishop and also at patterns of leadership in the local Church. Here we are concerned with the principle of collaborative leadership. This is a complex issue over which divisions are apparent in the Church at various levels. In the opinion of one writer, 'neither the simplicity of the concept of hierarchy nor an insufficiently thought out adoption of democratic forms of leadership will help us'.[10] The Church *is* different from other forms of human organisation, but that is no reason to put expectations on leaders of a superhuman kind. We shall consider later the focus and authority of the priesthood, but that is neither the beginning nor the end of the matter. The beginning was the collegial, corporate leadership of the early Church; the end for us today is a leadership properly responsive to the different demands made upon it. These include the liturgy, which requires a president; the decision-making process, which requires a chairman; and congregational oversight, which requires a pastor. There are no compelling reasons why the roles of president, chairman and pastor have to be combined, or why any of them may not be shared. Indeed, there are very good reasons, which will emerge later, why they should be undertaken by a collaborative ministry which inspires and enables the whole Church.

## (3) Collaboration between Local Churches

Just as the individual minister has a distorted view of his calling unless it is seen in relationship to the ministry of others (1 Corinthians 3.6), so local Churches can only fulfil their mission by recognising that it is shared with others. It should not be necessary to have formal team and group ministries before this is put into practice; parochial boundaries should express commitment to mission not a limitation of it. There are also other dimensions to mission which do not lend themselves to neat demarcation, involving Christians of other denominations in areas where the Church has no formal structures. This may make collaboration easier, but at the cost of distancing ministry from the institutional Church. The effect is serious unless local Churches can also learn to work in the same collaborative relationship. There are other ways, too, in which the local Church is weakened if it tries to live by its own resources alone. Further attention will be given to this later, but two other points will be made here about mission which are not simply related to the local Church.

69

## (4) Collaboration in Mission

The first is to observe that it is a false distinction to see the sphere of ordained ministry as being solely within the Church while that of lay ministry is specifically 'in the world'. Certainly there is a danger, as we have already noted, of consuming the energies of the laity within the organised activities of the Church. However this awareness should not obscure the contribution which each person has to make to the life of the Church:

> 'When each separate part works as it should, the whole body grows and builds itself up through love.' (Ephesians 4.16 GNB)

Similarly the public office of the ordained ministry means that many deacons and priests, and especially bishops, have an important contribution to make to the Church's mission. But there are problems about the priest who sees himself working 'out on the frontier', conducting a one-man mission which is unrelated to the rest of the Body of Christ. He, too, is called to a collaborative ministry. This leads to the second point, which is that no individual Christian is ever alone in witness to Christ. No matter how isolated the position may be, he or she acts in association with other Christians in the Body of Christ. In this sense every member of the Church is a representative minister. The basic resource of committed Christian men and women is by the grace of God everywhere present whether the Church develops a strategy or not. But they must be enabled to be the Church, and our consideration of a relevant strategy must therefore take us now to consider how such an enabling can take place.

NOTES TO CHAPTER 8: SHARED MINISTRY

[1] *PIM Report*, p.47, para.192, cf. paras. 84, 110.
[2] H. Oppenheimer, in *Stewards of the Mysteries of God*, ed. E. James, DLT, 1979, p.12.
[3] *Ibid.*, p.15f.
[4] *Report on the Position of the Laity in the Church*, 1902, 2nd edn. introd. by N. Sykes, 1952, p.iii.
[5] *The Documents of Vatican II*, ed. W. A. Abbott, Geoffrey Chapman, 1966, pp.491, 500.
[6] *Op.cit.*, p.31, para.110.
[7] 'Ministry and Ordination', in *The Final Report of the Anglican-Roman Catholic International Commission*, CTS/SPCK, 1982, p.30, para.3.
[8] *Ibid.*, p.33, para.7.
[9] R. Metcalfe, *Sharing Christian Ministry*, Mowbrays, 1981, p.7.
[10] J. J. A. Vollebergh, 'Religious leadership', in *Minister? Pastor? Prophet?*, SCM Press, 1980, p.55.

# 9: Basic Christian Communities

121.   In the previous chapter 'shared ministry' has been defined, not in terms of the laity giving a hand to the hard-pressed clergy, nor as the activity of ordinary Christians in their every-day witness, but as the way in which the ministry of Christ is continued through the Church. On this understanding, sharing in the common life *(koinonia)* is the means by which a true ministry *(diakonia)* is expressed. Those who meet to share in the apostolic teaching, the breaking of bread and the prayers are also called into a partnership of service (Acts 2.42, cf. 2 Corinthians 9.12f).

122.   Most members of the Church of England will associate these activities with their parish church. A call to 'shared ministry' will therefore seem to imply greater involvement in the work of the parish. It is the purpose of this chapter to demonstrate that this is only one way to share in the life of the Church. It will be suggested that there are three basic ways of participating in the common life in Christ. But first, the strengths and weaknesses of the familiar parochial system will be looked at in greater detail.

THE CONVERSION OF ENGLAND

123.   The two missionary movements which led to the conversion of the English in the seventh century were based on different strategies. That from Rome, led in the first phase by St Augustine and beginning in Kent, worked in co-operation with secular authority and infiltrated existing social structures. The Celtic mission from Iona, on the other hand, used monastic communities as spiritual power-bases for evangelistic forays into the heathen world. The contrast between these two approaches is remarkable in the differences of episcopal leadership. The Celtic bishop was a missionary figure who remained part of the religious community from which he originated. The Roman bishop in England became the chief spiritual adviser of the tribe among whom he resided. After a longish period of development during which the Roman strategy prevailed there emerged a settled pattern of pastoral care based on the tribal village. From the perspective of many centuries during which the English Church has continuously conducted its mission through the parochial system it may seem as though the alternative of 'minster-churches' *(monasteria)* from which groups of clergy travelled out into the surrounding area was no more than a transitory phase of development towards the establishment of a priest in each parish. It requires a great effort to imagine any alternative strategy to one based on the parochial system.

124.   There is nothing merely theoretical about the parochial system as the way in which the Church of England remains pastorally structured. As someone once expressed it in suitably pastoral language, there is not a blade of grass in the country which is not situated in somebody's parish. This arrangement may cover the ground very well, especially in those areas of the countryside which do actually contain blades of grass. But does it necessarily constitute the best way of ministering the Gospel in the highly urbanised society of modern Britain? There are at least six respects in which the parochial system has become *a weak instrument for mission.*

*(1) An Emphasis on Maintenance*

There is a constant tendency for the parish Church to experience a polarisation between maintenance and mission with the bias generally being towards the former, especially in those places where parish identity is strongest. The Gospel is so thoroughly 'earthed' in the parish that the continuing life of the community with its own inherited traditions easily governs the lifestyle of the Christian witness. It is true that there are discontinuities and fresh beginnings in the history of all communities and the parish Church can work through these. But its own congregation is often one of the most conservative elements in the social structure. The silent influence of ancient church and churchyard casts a ludicrous image of 'gimmickry' over any attempt to precipitate change. Not that effective mission will require the rejection of traditional ways in every situation, but all too often the parish Church is liable to become a refuge for those who appear in the community as lovers of traditionalism for its own sake. It is hard for the worshipper to realise that he or she is called to belong to a pilgrim people of God.

*(2) Meaningless Boundaries*

Once a centre of population grows to the point at which it has to be divided up by parochial boundaries considerable problems of identity are introduced. Rapid demographic changes in modern Britain mean that minor adjustments to boundary lines are quite insufficient. It is true that pastoral reorganisation is now much more readily available than in the past, but for most people in most town parishes the boundaries have little significance for any other than purely ecclesiastical purposes. The parish system remains best suited to tribal villages. Even in those circumstances where people are prepared to relate to whatever structures the Church has arranged (e.g. for marriage preparation, or for funerals) the parish boundaries are frequently a hindrance to the most effective pastoral use of such opportunities. The situation is even worse where new developments require new responses in the Church's mission. To take a not unusual circumstance: if a new housing estate is built on the edge of a town, partly in one country parish and partly in another, it will plainly be ridiculous for its inhabitants, who relate to each other and to the town, if they must find their Christian fellowship in separate village churches.

## (3) An Isolationist Style of Ministry

The very existence of boundary lines, whether sensible or not, promotes an isolationist view of ministry both on the part of the parochial clergy, and of congregations as well. It may be an inspiring thought that in its parish every local Church has its own mission field. In reality the hedges bordering the field only exist when looked at through ecclesiastical spectacles! The life of the town, and of its inhabitants, requires the building of much more complex and subtle relationships than are possible through a system of parochial units. Mission demands a collaborative style of ministry from the various parishes, and indeed from the various denominations, seeking to use their resources as effectively as possible. There is a double disadvantage in the fact that the same boundaries which determine the acknowledged 'mission field' of each local congregation often in the towns bear little relationship to the area from which these congregations are gathered. Many a comparatively strong urban congregation with a lively concern for mission and a good supply of capable lay leadership is attempting to conduct its mission in an area where perhaps relatively few of its congregation actually live. If residence is important for mission to be successful why is this state of affairs accepted? If residence is not essential, why is there not much more inter-church co-operation?

## (4) Staffing Shortages

Still, each parish is in the care of an incumbent or priest-in-charge, a fully-trained and authorised leader of the Church's mission. It is frequently pointed out in favour of the parochial system that it maintains the presence of clergy in deprived inner-city areas from which other professionals such as doctors, teachers and social workers, depart at the end of their working day. To achieve this, however, it is clear that a certain minimum supply of parochial clergy is needed. As we have seen, this has been assessed in recent years as a total of at least 11,600, but such an estimate clearly envisages the continued existence of many large parishes where it is difficult for the parish priest's 'cure of souls' to have much more than token significance for the majority of parishioners. The actual number of clergy available for parish work is now about 1,000 less than the minimum required. At the same time there are increasing opportunities for the clergy to be involved in specialist work offering scope for mission in areas where the Church's ministry has hitherto received little recognition, or is now wanted more than ever before. As a result the need to maintain a nationwide parochial system is seen by some as a restriction on the most effective deployment of the Church's stipendiary ministers. The position might be alleviated if stipendiaries could be withdrawn from parishes where there are well trained and experienced lay leaders and non-stipendiary ministers, but this seldom happens. Without a vigorous increase in the number of vocations to stipendiary ministry, and in the amount of money available to sustain it, there will be small chance of realising the full potential of the parochial system.

73

## (5) Few Links with Other Mission Agencies

For many people the parish church is a place of worship and social contact for those who wish to identify with the sort of people who belong. The very same 'unchurched' people who have this opinion may be in touch with and extremely appreciative of the various caring and mission agencies of the Church which operate through non-parochial channels. An example would be a refuge for battered wives, where the residents can be aware that it is run by 'the Church' and that the social worker is employed by 'the Church' but never begin to make a connection with the people who worship in the building on the street corner and who for their part never think that the refuge has much to do with them. There are of course shining instances where the local Church is very much the centre of outreach to the neighbourhood, but the fact of the situation is that a very great deal of effective mission is neither being channelled through the parochial system nor so engaged with it that the worship and mission of the Church are healthily interrelated.

## (6) Inability to Cope with Fragmented Communities

The theory that the Church ministers to the whole community through the parochial system must be radically questioned. It may be true that everybody lives in some parish or other, but for relatively few people does that place of residence circumscribe their entire lives. There is, for example, the enormously important area of the workplace, where human relationships, ethical issues, the structures of power and the decision-making processes all provide abundant scope for the ministry of the Gospel. At the very least it must be conceded that it is quite impossible, in view of the many 'fragmented' communities of the modern world, for the entire mission of the Church to be carried out by means of its parochial organisation alone.

THE STRENGTHS OF THE PAROCHIAL SYSTEM

125.   The foregoing considerations present a formidable case for the Church to develop alternative structures of mission. It is important now to add a mention of three *features which must not be lost* in any revision of the parochial system.

## (1) Availability of Pastoral Care

By means of the parochial system men and women in every place have known how to find the Church when they needed it. The Partners-in-Mission Consultation was perhaps inclined to exaggerate the distinction between mission and pastoral care. The Church of England has traditionally carried out its mission largely by means of pastoral work, with obvious benefits in terms of Christian nurture and the attractive witness of the common life in Christ. Within that framework there has been room for the evangelistic campaign, or the parish visitation. God's time in individual lives may not always coincide with the Church's outreach programme. There is a need for the Church and its ministry to be always there to provide continual witness and ready help. In this context a strategy of meeting the shortage of clergy by combining more and more parishes together is a strategy for decline.

## (2) Community Churches

There is also a strength in having a local Church committed to a particular neighbourhood. Non-parochial patterns produce 'associational churches' which are defined more in terms of membership than of mission. It is vital to have an associational element (i.e. commitment on the part of those who belong) and a Church which merely reflects the life-style of the community in which it is situated has betrayed the Gospel. There is, however, another betrayal of the Gospel in failure to witness to what it has to say about social issues as well as its ability to fulfil individual need. The parish Church is there because the parish is there, not because it attracts a large enough congregation to keep in business. In practice, however, the concerns of the congregation it does have may not match the needs of the parish and then the parish Church belies both its name and its purpose.

## (3) The Public Face of the Church

With the establishment of an increasing number of non-parochial ministries connections with the parish Churches must be maintained. The parochial ministry is sometimes referred to as just one among a number of sector ministries, with the particular task of ministering to people where they live in residential communities, and with special reference to their family relationships. What used to be all-embracing now relates to a part of life only. This is wholly inadequate as an understanding of the significance of the parish Church. It is not to be defined as merely the neighbourhood sector of the Christian mission. It is here that we find the public, open door of the Church through which any and all may enter. It is the local and visible expression of the Church catholic. Within its walls all ages and types and intellects are challenged to work out their common membership in Christ. The healthy life of the parish Church ensures that what we find elsewhere in society is the substantial Body of Christ and not some indefinable, ghostly Christian presence.

THE KOINONIA OF LARGE AND SMALL GROUPS

126.   How can the strengths of this inheritance be retained if the restrictive and isolationist features of the parochial system are removed? It is often pointed out that membership of the average parish Church fails to bestow the benefits of either the very large or the very small group. If it has a congregation numbered in hundreds it will be described as 'impersonal'; yet a congregation of thousands at a Church congress or cathedral festival occasion would be termed 'inspiring' or 'uplifting', rather than 'impersonal'. Similarly, a handful of people scattered around a parish church on Sunday morning is depressing, whereas the same number in somebody's home is intimate and encouraging. Reflection on this state of affairs has led some

reformers to suggest replacing the parochial system with a network of house churches which come together regularly for large-scale conferences and acts of worship. This solution has the disadvantage that it concentrates on the needs of the individual for helpful relationships, while abandoning some of the strengths and accentuating some of the weaknesses of the existing system.

CELL, CONGREGATION AND PILGRIMAGE

127.   This strategy suggests three levels at which *koinonia* is apparent as an expression of the life of the catholic Church. Parish Churches are retained for congregations which have a defined area of commitment to ministry, within which public worship and pastoral care are available to all. From these centres it is not just individuals who pray:

'Send us out
in the power of your Spirit
to live and work
to your praise and glory.'

It is the life and work of Christian cells in the community which are designed to overcome some of the weaknesses in the missionary capability and individual care of the parish Church. Some cells would be house groups within the parish, related to the pastoral structure of the congregation. Other cells would be involved in community projects, in work among down-and-outs, in housing associations, in running bookshops; some would be prayer groups. The third type of cell would be the Church's witness in industry, commerce, education, medicine and government.

128.   In addition to the congregation and the cell there would be a regular large assembly of the Church. The occasional and variable nature of this gathering would emphasise the transitory staging-posts of the pilgrim people of God, who find on earth 'no continuing city'. The cathedral as a centre of pilgrimage and the mother church of the diocese is the natural focus. However, there may be additional centres of historic Christian worship used for this purpose; there may be deanery events; and there may be occasions when there is cause for celebration at one particular parish church.

THE LOCAL CHURCH

129.   In this report the term 'local Church' is used regularly. The responsibility of the local Church for ministry is one of the key ideas behind the strategy. It is therefore important to be clear what is intended by reference to it. It has three aspects.

130.   In the first instance the local Church is the public congregation mentioned above. It would possess a parish, that is a geographical area within which it would be responsible for mission and for providing such

pastoral ministry as is expected from the parish Church at present. However, the local Church would not be in the care of a parish priest, but of a leadership team consisting of local ministers and others working on a diocesan basis. This will be enlarged upon in later chapters, but the significance must be noted here of the regular convening of this local congregation for public worship. This is the local manifestation of the catholic Church. It therefore bears responsibility for witnessing to the Gospel in its own locality, but the boundary lines of the parish, while possessing legal significance in respect of parishioners' rights, would not represent absolute demarcation in terms of the Church's mission. For the latter purpose a broader definition of the local Church is necessary, corresponding to the present deanery.

131.   Deaneries are units of synodical government in the Church. They should also be used as units of co-operation in mission and related to definable areas of the community in which they are situated.[1] This might mean considerable variation in the size of a deanery. One of the conclusions drawn from our examination both of rural and of urban ministry in Chapters 3 and 4 was that a need exists for parishes to draw on educational and ministerial resources which can be shared by the whole deanery. It is through the deanery structures that the local Church can most effectively make use of diocesan ministry teams. Moreover, the development of ecumenical relationships and action offers more scope on a deanery basis.

132.   Thirdly, the cells which have been described above need to be related to both parish congregation and deanery. This is shown in diagrammatic form in Appendix 3.

133.   The local Church is therefore envisaged here as at one and the same time the deanery, the public congregation and the cell. There need be no confusion, because it simply means seeing the Church organised locally in different ways for different purposes. Its components may be listed as follows:

i) the deanery synod, with a clearly briefed deanery mission committee (this would replace existing deanery pastoral committees);

ii) a diocesan ministry team of priests and deacons working with the deanery mission committee;

iii) a certain number of public congregations, each with a parochial area and church council, and a leadership team or eldership (as described in Chapter 15 below); and

iv) a certain number of cells, some of which would be directly related to the deanery mission committee, and some of which would be units of the parochial congregations.

134.   There is a theological definition of the local Church which equates it with the diocese, the point being that the Bishop represents the local Church to the wider Church and *vice versa*. This is an important part of the Bishop's office, but in practice few people think of a diocese as a local Church, or use the term in that way. There is a degree of absurdity about the manner in which the function of the diocese is sometimes advocated along these lines. In any case the theory fails to take seriously the implications of an early historical development in the episcopate which is described in the WCC Lima document as follows: 'Bishops began increasingly to exercise *episkope* over several local communities at the same time.'[2] For our purpose this development is important. It enables us to distinguish between the functions and responsibilities of the local Church on the one hand and of the diocese on the other. It is on the conjunction and right relation of these two that this strategy is based, and from which the ministry of the Bishop acquires its particular significance.

NOTES TO CHAPTER 9: BASIC CHRISTIAN COMMUNITIES

[1] For proposals on how this might be done see: *The Church of England and Contemporary Communities* – A Working Paper by the Church and Community Unit of the Brunel Institute of Organisation and Social Studies, March 1978. See also, C. Handy, *The Rural Deanery and its Future*, St George's House Paper No.3, July 1981; and G. Stamp, 'Does the Deanery make a difference?', *Crucible*, Oct.–Dec. 1982, pp.149–54.
[2] *BEM*, p.24, para.21.

## 10: Responsibility and Partnership

135.  All that has been considered so far concerning the ministry of the whole people of God may be summarised by the two words, *responsibility* and *partnership*. The individual Christian is called through baptism to belong to a fellowship of service. Responsibility for witness to the Gospel rests equally upon every member of this fellowship, but it is a responsibility which is discharged through partnership, so that no member can say of another, 'I have no need of you' (1 Corinthians 12.21).

THE MINISTRY ROLL

136.  This inclusive understanding of the ministry of the Body of Christ has already led to a suggestion that there should be a 'ministry roll' in each local Church of all those who are prepared to express their baptismal commitment in an appropriate context (see Chapter 7). It would be a denial of its very purpose to see this as the definition of a narrow in-group or ministerial elite. Its function would be to challenge every Church member to take their baptism seriously, and to realise that through baptism they have already received all the authorisation that is necessary for them to act as lay ministers of Christ. This ministry gathers up the prayers of the housebound and the practical help of the good neighbour who gives 'a cup of cold water' for Christ's sake, just as much as the work of those who teach the faith or are called to positions of leadership in the Church. Above all, this partnership should be seen as a way of fulfilling Christ's ministry in the market place and the council chamber; the office, the classroom and the psychiatric ward; on the stage and on the shop floor.

137.  Those who are called to lay service in the secular world speak often of their isolation, and lack of support from their fellow Christians who expect them to be busy in Church-based activities during their spare time. It is easy for them to resent this lack of understanding, and to forget the necessity of partnership in their ministry. It is for this reason that work-based cells should be an important element in the mission of the local Church. The individual Christian who accepts responsibility for witness to Christ needs also to accept the Church as God's gift to maintain him or her in true service. None realised this more acutely than the members of the 'Confessing Church' in pre-war Nazi Germany. As their spokesman, Dietrich Bonhoeffer was moved to write:

> 'It is easily forgotten that the fellowship of Christian brethren is a gift of grace, a gift of the kingdom of God that any day may be taken from us, that the time that still separates us from utter loneliness may be brief indeed. Therefore, let him who

until now has had the privilege of living a common Christian life with other Christians praise God's grace from the bottom of his heart. Let him thank God on his knees and declare: It is grace, nothing but grace.'[1]

## THE NEEDS AND RESOURCES OF THE LOCAL CHURCH

138.   What applies to the individual Christian applies also to the local Church in all three of its aspects described in the last chapter. It has a responsibility to witness to the Good News of Jesus Christ; it can fulfil this responsibility only in partnership with others. This involves ecumenical co-operation through parochial and deanery structures to achieve a united ministry in the setting up of cells for different purposes.

139.   The local Church also needs the partnership of the diocese. Through a process of consultation with each deanery mission committee and PCC the Bishop would gain a picture of the needs and resources for ministry in each place. As a result a strategy for ministry in each diocese could be developed to enable the Bishop to fulfil his own responsibilities for seeing that ministry is provided where it is needed. No doubt most dioceses already give a great deal of attention to strategic questions concerning the best use of stipendiary ministers. This has become a necessity in dioceses where considerable changes have had to be made to meet Sheffield targets. Some dioceses also take into account the existence of non-stipendiary priests and have developed clear policies for their ministry, although the 1983 NSM report has shown that so far their availability has not much affected schemes for pastoral re-organisation. What this strategy proposes is a diocesan ministry policy which also takes into account the ministerial resources of each local Church, and does so not just on the basis of impressions or even of statistics, but through a process of detailed consultations. Regular reviews with a diocesan consultant would then enable each local Church to identify changes in its needs and resources as they occurred. The process would ensure that what was felt to be important locally was seen in the perspective of the Church's mission throughout the diocese. The training of stipendiary ministers would prepare them to engage in this process of consultation between the diocese and the local Church, and it would be an important part of their ministry to set this forward in each place. The aim is that 'any living local church should be living not just parochially but also from the knowledge and strength of the wider Church'.[2]

NOTES TO CHAPTER 10: RESPONSIBILITY AND PARTNERSHIP

[1]D. Bonhoeffer, *Life Together*, SCM Press, ET 1954, p.9f.
[2]M. Hollings, *Hearts not Garments: Christ is our Peace*, DLT, 1982, p.65f.

# 11. Orders and the Recognition of Gifts

140.  In this section on the ministry of the whole people of God 'shared ministry' has been interpreted not as a way of rallying to the aid of the clergy, but as a response to the calling of all who are baptised into Christ to act as his Body in the world. The world is the sphere of Christ's ministry, where the Church is called to be active in his service. This takes priority over running the Church's organisation. However, a crucial distinction has been drawn between running the Church and being the Church. The alternative to self-contained ecclesiastical activities is not meant to be the dispersed and lonely witness of individual Christians. Everywhere the Church equips itself for its mission by becoming shaped into the fellowship of the Holy Spirit, using for this purpose the gifts which the Spirit gives for ministry in the Church.

141.  These gifts are to be found in every member of Christ's Body: indeed, in an important biblical sense each person *is* a gift of the Spirit (cf. Ephesians 4.11). No amount of planning can arrange the occurrence of these gifts. The life of the Church differs from that of other institutions in that it depends at the end of the day, not upon strategies and organisation, but upon the response it makes to this divine provision. It must therefore be a matter of priority to ensure that gifts for ministry are appropriately recognised and exercised. This has to be done with imagination. The danger is that too narrow an understanding of Christian ministry will be applied to God's manifold gifts. The ministry of the Word, for example, is not limited to sermons from the pulpit, vitally necessary though this form of it certainly is. Other ways of ministering the Word include, paradoxically, holding one's tongue (Ephesians 4.29), as well as a life lived in obedience to the Word, a gift of listening to others, and the inspiration of prophecy, of exhortation, and of encouragement.

142.  From this perspective ministry is not a problem to be solved; it is a profound source of joy as God is found to be at work. In its worship, the Church offers a sacrifice of thanksgiving for God's supreme gift of himself. How can there be anything lacking in ministry if we can say:

'The Lord is here: his Spirit is with us'?

Indeed, the Christian assembly for worship is the place where the Lord commissions his servants, and where they receive power as the Holy Spirit comes upon them.

143.   This picture of a lay and (in the broadest sense) charismatic ministry will be inadequate if it leaves out of account what history has shown to be necessary, namely, that the Church has to give order and shape to its ministry. Without these the identification of the institution with the Gospel it proclaims is always in danger of becoming uncertain. Furthermore, many in the Church believe that what has proved to be an historical necessity has been divinely ordered in advance. The threefold ministry of bishops, priests and deacons has retained important aspects of the ministry of Christ and is held to be the divine pattern for Church order, forming in fact part of God's gift of ministry in the Church. Others who would not accept the threefold order as quite so normative are nevertheless prepared to agree with the WCC Lima document that it 'may serve today as an expression of the unity we seek and also as a means for achieving it'.[1]

144.   Without showing much sign of wishing to abandon the threefold order of ministry the Church of England has nevertheless over the past century or so developed various new forms of officially recognised ministry in a way which suggests that a process of re-ordering is taking place. Deaconesses, licensed lay workers, readers and evangelists (Church Army officers are admitted by the Archbishop of Canterbury to the office of evangelist) have all received a form of national accreditation. In some dioceses there are other authorised ministers as well, for example lay elders, or pastoral assistants. None of these categories, apart from deaconesses, are described as orders, but the distinctions are obscure apart from the highly personal one of an order requiring lifelong commitment.

145.   What has happened, in effect, is that the threefold ministry of bishops, priests and deacons has become part of a spectrum of ministry running through the whole Church which challenges the rigid distinction between clergy and laity but leaves the concept of orders without any precision. Stimulation of the ministry of the laity provokes a demand for training, which in turn receives recognition by some form of accreditation, and this results in less and less certainty over why some are ordained. The most recent report in the Church of England on the theology of ordination even suggested that 'it is not improper that the drawing of the line between ordained and not-ordained be left somewhat blurred'.[2] Rather than extending ordination to include new forms of authorised ministry, the report preferred to see:

> 'a spectrum of ministry which ranges from the Holy Orders or Distinctive Ministry at one end, through other permanent ministries and the more occasional charismatic ministries to the ministry of all Christian people at the other.'[3]

Helpful as this is in extending the Church's understanding of ministry it leaves no basis other than long-established custom for drawing the line between ordained and lay ministry where it is, with its enormous consequences for synodical government, canon law, appointment to benefices, and the rest.

## THE THEOLOGY OF ORDERS

146.   This is an awkward moment for producing a working definition of orders in the Church of England. The failure of the Covenanting proposals in 1982 revealed a weakness at this point which has prompted some work on the theology to be put in hand. At the same time two important ecumenical documents in this field have recently been published, and the Church of England is now preparing its response. These are: the *Final Report* of the Anglican-Roman Catholic International Commission (ARCIC), containing among other material the earlier statement of 1973 on 'Ministry and Ordination' together with the subsequent elucidations of 1979; and the long-awaited World Council of Church's document, *Baptism, Eucharist and Ministry (BEM)*. With such important discussions in process I can hardly offer here a comprehensive theological statement. Within the area relating to the authorisation of specific forms of ministry in the Church I must, however, take a clear view.

147.   The WCC document expresses concisely the key question in considering the place of orders:

'How, according to the will of God and under the guidance of the Holy Spirit, is the life of the Church to be understood and ordered, so that the Gospel may be spread and the community built up in love?'[4]

The traditional answer to this question has put a heavy emphasis, not upon the threefold order, but upon the priesthood. In fact the threefold order has been seen as really but one order, that of the clergy, within which a hierarchy exists. It is this ordained ministry *as a whole* which is described in *BEM* as a priesthood. In the FOAG report deacons are regarded as but incipient presbyters:

'It is true that there are certain presbyteral functions which a deacon may not perform, just as there are certain episcopal functions which a presbyter may not perform, but it is nonetheless a single priestly ministry in which all three orders share in different ways.'[5]

The resulting pattern of ordained ministry has been criticised as 'a grossly inflated type of priesthood cramped with the monopoly of most other ministries'.[6]

148.   There is a link between this view of orders and the model of the Church as the flock of God over which Christ has appointed pastors to shepherd it; so a hierarchical pattern emerges:

| Chief Pastors | = | Bishops |
| Pastors | = | Presbyters |
| Apprentice Pastors | = | Deacons |
| Flock | = | Laity |

Although a pattern of pastoral oversight is both biblical and essential to the welfare of the Church, this type of hierarchy is inadequate for two reasons. First it does not do justice to the distinctive ministries signified by the threefold order; secondly, as the ACCM Report *Ordained Ministry Today* expressed it:

> 'It is a limitation of the image of pastor that—as an image of oversight—it leaves no room for a growth to maturity and participation by the sheep.'[7]

149.   Other biblical models of the Church are available, and the one which has often been used to support the development of 'every-member' ministry has been that of the Body of Christ filled with the Holy Spirit. This allows for a necessary and continuing tension between order and creativity in the Church's ministry. True creativity occurs through a variety of 'charisms'— i.e. 'the gifts bestowed by the Holy Spirit on any member of the body of Christ for the building up of the community and the fulfilment of its calling'.[8] It is not for the Church to order these 'charisms', which are 'the work of one and the same Spirit, distributing them separately to each individual at will' (1 Corinthians 12.11). On the other hand, they must be acknowledged as God's gifts to the Church for its ministry:

> 'In order to enhance their effectiveness the community will recognise publicly certain of these charisms.'[9]

GIFTS AND ORDERS

150.   Although the orders of bishops, priests and deacons in themselves may be seen as gifts of ministry to the Church, because all true ministry is from God, nevertheless it is clear that among the many individuals who are called into ordained ministry there exists a wide range of 'charisms'. The significance of this for the work of ordained ministers will be developed in the following chapters. Here it is important to emphasize that the different orders do not distinguish between different 'charisms': there are no separate *orders* of teachers, pastors, evangelists, administrators, still less of prophets. 'Charisms', as gifts of the Spirit, may not be so ordered, merely recognised when they appear. Orders exist for a separate purpose.

151.   Orders exist to be a representative focus of the Church's authority to minister the Gospel in Christ's name. The ordained ministry is therefore composed of members of the laity who are authorised to represent the whole Church, both in their public ministry and in their representative functions within the Christian community. The Bishop is the key 'ministry of order' within the Church. He is an 'overseer', responsible for the welfare of the

84

whole Body. To fulfil this task, he works in association with a college of presbyters (or elders, or priests) who share in his pastoral and teaching ministry. They participate in presiding at the Eucharist and thus relate the local Church to the wider Church in this focus of unity. Deacons also assist the Bishop in supplying the needs of the Church and serving the community on behalf of the whole Church. As representative ministers, bishops are a sign of the apostolate of the laity; priests are a sign of the priesthood of all believers; deacons are a sign of the call to servanthood of all who are 'in Christ'. Thus each separate order has a distinctive ministry, which is at the same time clearly related to the other orders and able to include within itself a wide variety of 'charisms'.

152.   It is now possible, in the context of the ministry of the whole people of God, to look more closely at the work of bishops, priests and deacons, and then to turn to those resources which are available wherever two or three meet in Christ's name, the gifts of the Spirit, which require no other authorisation beyond baptism.

NOTES TO CHAPTER 11: ORDERS AND THE RECOGNITION OF GIFTS

[1] *BEM*, p.24, para. 22.
[2] *The Theology of Ordination:* A Report by the Faith and Order Advisory Group of the Board for Mission and Unity, GS 281, 1975, p.17, para.46.
[3] *Ibid.*, p.19, para.49.
[4] *BEM*, p.20f., para.6.
[5] GS 281, p.15, para.39.
[6] Marcel Boivin, in *Pro Mundi Vita*, April 1982, p.2.
[7] *Ordained Ministry Today—A Discussion of Its Nature and Role*, ACCM, 1969, p.37.
[8] *BEM*, p.21, para.7.
[9] *Ibid.*, p.27, para.32.

# THE STRATEGY – 2
# PARTICULAR KINDS
# OF MINISTRY

# 12: The Bishop

153.   Recent debates in the General Synod have shown that, just as there is an urgent need for the Church of England to clarify its theology of ministry and priesthood following its failure to accept the Covenanting proposals, so too there is a need for an investigation of its understanding of episcopacy.[1] The need is perhaps felt for two reasons. One is that the Church of England has been in the habit of making certain rather definite theological statements about the role of the Bishop which singularly fail to match up to current practice. For example, he is seen as a focus of unity, when in the past bishops have presided over the fragmentation of the Church and their successors today must work within the limitations of our continuing disunity. Is the focus therefore lost, or does the theory require re-interpretation? As one recent writer on the episcopate has asked: 'Is the measure of unity which we have not got a condemnation of ourselves, of our system, or of our history?'[2] Again, it is fundamental to regard the Bishop's office as one of pastoral oversight, but it is not easy for one man to provide an intimate and personal pastoral ministry in a diocese of the present average size. Clearly there are disadvantages in multiplying dioceses across the land, reproducing in the process their synodical and administrative infrastructure. We therefore create new suffragan bishoprics (there were none in 1870; there are now 62) and seek to revise our understanding of shared oversight to explain this development.

154.   There is, then, a concern to develop an *orthopraxis* of episcopacy which will in turn lead to a contemporary theology of episcopacy. Secondly, there is also a pressure on the Bishops themselves to find some organising principles around which, with the assent of the Church at large, they can seek to order their priorities amid the vast range of conflicting demands which are made upon them. The Lambeth Conference of 1978 well illustrated, in its Report, the extent of these demands without providing the necessary systematisation. The following is an anthology of quotations from the Report:

a) 'A bishop is called to be one with the apostles in proclaiming Christ's resurrection and interpreting the Gospel, and to testify to Christ's sovereignty.'

b) 'He will give major attention to his public ministry.'

c) 'He will have a concern for the well-being of the whole community.'

d) 'The bishop should be ready to be present in secular situations...'

e) '...to give time to the necessary study...'
f) 'to take sides publicly if necessary...about issues which concern justice, mercy and truth.'
g) 'The bishop's authority is interpreted and expressed...through his leadership and participation in the synods and councils of the Church.'
h) 'The guardianship of the faith is a collegial responsibility of the episcopate.'
i) 'The bishop is the sign and agent of unity and continuity within the diocese and within the whole Church.'
j) 'The bishop is primarily a father in God to his diocese.'
k) 'The bishop represents also the apostleship of Christ and as such he ordains to the ministry of the Church.'
l) 'The primary function of the bishop is to minister in and to the Church.'
m) 'It is also his function to teach.'
n) '...his function of exercising pastoral care over his diocese.'
o) '...his own pastoral care of his clergy.'
p) 'The bishop represents his individual diocese within the Church of God in his meetings with his fellow bishops.'
q) 'He represents the universal episcopate to his own people.'
r) '(He) is at once the focus and symbol of the catholicity of the Church.'
s) 'It is the function of the bishop to exercise a prophetic ministry to the world.'
t) 'The function of a bishop...does not cease with his personal ministry of ordaining, preaching, teaching, pastoral oversight, and public pronouncements. It extends also to the oversight of these functions in the diocese at large.'
u) 'The bishop is deeply concerned with evangelisation in his diocese.'
v) 'The bishop's office is to be the chief liturgical minister in his diocese.'[3]

155.    In the face of this daunting description of their task (which does not include mention of administration and committee work, nor of the national responsibilities of the Bishops which have a peculiar significance in the Church of England) the Lambeth Fathers recommended a proper programme of training for episcopal ministry. The fifth meeting of the Anglican Consultative Council, held at Newcastle-upon-Tyne in 1981, drew attention to the need for the Bishops to have the assistance of consultants and support groups. Training and support are admirable, but they will not remedy the defects of an unrealistic job description.

A THREEFOLD EPISCOPAL ROLE

156.    In this strategy it is suggested that the ministry of the Bishop comes under three heads: he is responsible for pastoral oversight (*episcope*); he provides a focus of unity; and he commends the apostolic faith.

## (1) The Bishop's Responsibility for Pastoral Oversight

'*Bishops* preach the Word, preside at the sacraments, and administer discipline in such a way as to be representative pastoral ministers of oversight...They have pastoral oversight of the area to which they are called.'[4]

Every Christian is required to give care to others of a pastoral kind. As Sir Thomas More put it: 'God hath given to every man cure and charge of his neighbour.' This is the calling of the good Samaritan. Pastoral oversight is more specific; it concerns the welfare of the Church, which is the responsibility of many people in different ways, in different parts of the Church's life, and among different groups. Oversight of the Church *as a whole* is committed to the ordained ministry:

'There are some whom the Holy Spirit commissions through ordination for service to the whole community...This pastoral authority belongs primarily to the bishop.'[5]

The Bishop's concern is to safeguard the fellowship and witness of the whole Christian community, and also to undertake the 'cure of souls' of all who belong to his flock. In both of these aspects pastoral oversight is essentially personal. It is therefore necessary for presbyters to be associated with the Bishop in caring for each local eucharistic community. But the Bishop is also 'pastor pastorum' and a great deal of his time and attention must be occupied in the ordination, appointment and support of his priests and deacons for their spheres of ministry. Pastoral care of the clergy is not something the Bishop has to think about only when things are going wrong. Each minister needs to be aware of his or her place in the Bishop's provision of ministry in the diocese, to have opportunities to review the development of their work, and to assess personal growth in ministry with a proper consideration of in-service training requirements.

The Bishop's objective in this pastoral care is to reaffirm the vocation of each man and woman to be a minister of the Gospel. He is in no position to shoulder this burden alone; nor is it wise, in view of his involvement in the making of appointments, for him to expect to be an all-sufficient support for each one. It is his duty to see that alternative consultants and support groups are available and that a structure of consultation exists. A bishop quickly discovers that the effective organisation of pastoral care involves constant attention to administration and management. This is an important reason why it is unrealistic to suppose it is possible to increase the number of dioceses while expecting much of the administration to be done at regional level. It is also a false distinction to see the Bishop's role as one of pastoral relationship rather than management. Management is an aspect of human relationships in which the Bishop needs to develop some skills, since it is impossible for him to avoid it; his objective should be management in the service of the Gospel.

## (2) The Bishop as a Focus of Unity

From the earliest emergence of the monarchical episcopate the importance of the Bishop's role as a focus of unity has been emphasized. This has three aspects: in his person he represents Christ's headship of the Church; the unity of the Body is expressed through his presidency of the eucharistic fellowship; and the unity of the catholic Church is maintained through the mutual communion and conference of the Bishops of each local Christian community. There are important points here in building the case for episcopacy as the right system of Church order to be entertained in ecumenical schemes for reunion. But the very need for reunion schemes illustrates the point that episcopacy can only focus a unity which already exists. Nevertheless, as a symbol it is not entirely without power, since the Bishop of an English diocese does in fact provide a focus for a considerable number of eucharistic fellowships (he is hardly on a par with the *episcopi vagantes!*), and he is also in a position to promote the unity which his office symbolises:

'As a focus of the unity of the Church, in the present divided Christendom, he should be a leader in ecumenical affairs in his diocese.'[6]

Moreover, the Bishop is still able, within the limitations of the divided Churches, to represent the universal Church to the local Church and *vice versa*.

### (3) The Bishop's Apostolic Mission

The Bishop's role is both at the centre and at the periphery of the Church. The office brings particular opportunities for mission, and these are increased because of the national recognition given to the Church of England. One diocesan bishop considers that he has never had so secular a job as that of his present post. There are endless opportunities to represent the Church, and therefore Christ as Lord of the Church; to be a public spokesman for the Church, and therefore for the Gospel; to become acquainted with people bearing heavy responsibility in public life, and therefore to do the work of an evangelist. Where a bishop has time to develop these contacts he is of all Christian ministers the one best placed to bring together the institutional Church and the outreach of pioneering ministries, so that the two are not separated and moving in different directions. In providing ministry within the diocese through his priests and deacons the Bishop is not meeting pastoral needs alone; these colleagues share his apostolic task, which includes making new Christians, and teaching and interpreting the faith of the apostles.

BISHOPS AND SHARED MINISTRY

157. Any semblance of order which may be introduced into the many conflicting demands upon a bishop's time and attention will not alter the fact that the expectations placed upon him are great. These are only partly due to the size of the average diocese in the Church of England. Indeed the pressures may be greater in a smaller diocese, with less technical expertise available, a smaller central administrative service, and less flexibility in making appointments. Shared ministry has therefore been a necessity for

bishops for much longer than the Church has been aware of the corresponding limitations of a one-man, omnicompetent parochial ministry. The Bishop's pastoral oversight is shared with the parish priest; his care of the clergy with the archdeacon, and informally with the rural dean. He surrounds himself with legal officers, examining chaplains, directors of ordinands, training officers, and advisers on this and that. As guardian and teacher of the faith the Bishop needs theological consultants; in his public ministry he needs advisers with specialist knowledge of economic, social, political and educational issues; in his concern for evangelism the Bishop may appoint a diocesan missioner. All of this certainly amounts to shared ministry at a diocesan level. However, in addition there has developed over the last century in the great majority of dioceses a shared episcopal ministry; that is to say, suffragan bishops have been appointed to share the distinctively episcopal functions (confirmations, ordinations, institutions), and also the care of the clergy, and the chairmanship of some committees. Beginning in 1870 this modern revival of suffragan bishoprics has grown now to sixty-two in total, during a period when the number of dioceses has been increased from twenty-five to forty-four. The Church of England is now unique in the Anglican Communion in possessing more suffragans than diocesans. This development in the Church's ministry has not received universal approval:

> 'The position of suffragan bishops is not one that should be further developed or maintained. They have not enabled episcopacy to shine with a primitive light.'[7]

HOW MANY BISHOPS PER DIOCESE?

158.   The basic fault with suffragan bishops, according to their opponents, is that they are a theological anomaly. This is because the Bishop ceases to be a focus of unity if he exists in plurality; and moreover, the unity of the Church which he represents must be expressed in territorial terms such as a diocese. A suffragan bishop, despite his title, does not replace the territorial jurisdiction of the diocesan in any part of the diocese. To do this a formal area scheme is necessary.

> 'This transforms a monarchical episcopate with episcopal curates (suffragans or auxiliaries) into an episcopal team with the diocesan as chairman.'[8]

This is considered more satisfactory, but theory and practice still do not meet, because it is argued that an area bishopric *is*, theologically speaking, a diocese and should be recognised as such. The case against suffragan bishops is a serious one because their present numbers indicate that they are bearing the main weight of episcopal ministry in many of its aspects. Should they continue to exist? It must be admitted that there is something very singular about the idea of the Bishop in relation to his diocese, and we have used the singular hitherto in this report. Further reflection, however, suggests a modification of the strict 'one Bishop per diocese' principle.

159.   The WCC Lima text points out that originally the bishop was the leader of a single eucharistic community, and it adds: 'In this context the

bishop's ministry was a focus of unity within the whole community.' Subsequent development made the Bishop leader of the Church in an area comprising several eucharistic communities. In this situation the presbyters, through their association with the Bishop, provided the focus of unity in the individual communities.[9] It was therefore decided centuries ago that the unity of the Church does not require expression through a one-man ministry. If the most essential function of the Bishop in his ministry as a focus of unity, namely his presidency of the Eucharist, may be shared with others, there seems to be no overriding reason why his other functions may not also be shared.

EPISCOPAL TEAM MINISTRIES

160.   A geographical sharing of responsibilities is not the only possible advantage of episcopal team ministries in each diocese. By this means a wider range of gifts can be brought to the fulfilment of the demanding brief described at the Lambeth Conference. Area schemes have an advantage over the multiplication of smaller dioceses in that they are flexible enough to permit different styles of leadership to be incorporated in a common episcopate. Different members of the team can relate to different aspects of life in the community. An example can also be given by the Bishops of co-operation between different traditions of churchmanship. This means, of course, that each is accepted as a Bishop of the whole diocese rather than being in any way a minister to churches of one tradition in particular. A corporate episcopate of this kind may well wish to divide the diocese into geographical areas of responsibility, but, as in the case of parochial team ministries at present, this should not prevent sharing of work in other ways throughout the diocese. In extending the idea of episcopal collegiality within dioceses, the report *Bishops and Dioceses* produced the definition that 'the college of bishops is the bishop of the diocese'.[10] One reaction to this is that people want a Father-in-God, not a committee; but what loaded words these are! In pastoral terms, do even the present suffragan bishops fail to be Fathers-in-God? In theological terms, what does the cry for one Father of us all have to say about maturity in Christ, of whom there are many icons? In organisational terms, does an episcopal team have to behave like a committee any more than it is necessary for a presbyteral team to behave like one? It would be wrong to develop the idea of collegiality within the diocese into a new doctrine of episcopacy. It is seen as one possible pattern which is already receiving some expression. In Chapter 17 it will be argued that in fact there are three different patterns which could be applied to the variety of dioceses existing at present. In what follows here we shall continue to speak of the Bishop (single or corporate) in his provision of ministry within the diocese through the other orders associated with him.

## NOTES TO CHAPTER 12: THE BISHOP

[1]See e.g. the debate in February 1983 on *Episcopacy and the Role of the Suffragan Bishop*, A Report by the Dioceses Commission, GS 551.

[2]Peter Moore, 'The Anglican Episcopate, its strengths and limitations', in *Bishops—But What Kind?*, Reflections on Episcopacy collected and edited by P. Moore, SPCK, 1982, p.134.

[3]*The Report of the Lambeth Conference 1978*, CIO, 1978, pp.44, 77f., 94f.

[4]*BEM*, p.26, para.29.

[5]ARCIC, *The Final Report*, p.53f., para.5 of the Statement on Authority in the Church.

[6]*Bishops and Dioceses*, The Report of the Ministry Committee Working Party on the Episcopate, ACCM, 1971, p.11.

[7]P. Moore, *op.cit.*, p.172.

[8]*Ibid.*

[9]See *BEM*, p.24, paras.20f.

[10]*Op.cit.*, p.26.

## 13: The Priests

161. One of the most remarkable changes concerning the ministry of the Church of England since Leslie Paul wrote his report has been the spread of an almost paralysing uncertainty about the proper role of the clergyman. This has not resulted directly from the increasing emphasis on the ministry of the laity which has already been described. It has more to do with the changed position of the Church in society, and the consequent decline in the status and influence of the clergy. Of course this is a process which has been going on for much longer than the last twenty years. But the Anglican clergy have been part of a traditional social structure which has not been seriously shaken until the last twenty years, even though the signs of disintegration have been apparent since the First World War. The modern clergyman has behind him a history of development almost without parallel in any other occupation. Dr Anthony Russell has clearly demonstrated in his book, *The Clerical Profession*, that the model of the Anglican clergyman which is at present being taken from us is one which may be described as professional, not in modern terms, but rather of an otherwise extinct Victorian type.[1]

162. The uncertainties which have resulted from this erosion of professional status have been further increased by the diminishing area reserved for ordained ministry within the Church. In their desire to encourage the ministry of the laity, bishops have given licences and authorisation to lay people to preach, to teach, to administer the Holy Communion, to visit the sick, to bury the dead, to undertake all kinds of pastoral ministry. A reductionist attitude is now sometimes expressed which defines the distinctive ministry of a priest as limited to a few parts of the Eucharist, and perhaps the giving of absolution and benediction. An identity crisis has arisen for the Church's ordained ministry, not so much because the laity have 'usurped' the functions of the clergy, but because the steep decline in the number of clergy has led to an unbalanced emphasis upon those aspects of their ministry which are regarded as inalienable. Peter Coleman has pointed out what this can do, for example, to the vocation of a rural priest:

> 'It is miserable for a mission or pastorally minded minister to take services in lieu of knowing the people, and it puts an unbalancing emphasis on celebrating the sacraments as the main Christian task. Furthermore, the expensively trained and supported full-time minister is presumed to have the best resources for teaching and preaching...whereas presiding at the Eucharist and other Sunday services is well within the competence of lay people, who in the working week earn a living at far more complex tasks.'[2]

It is difficult to claim that the Church of England is now using such clergy as it does possess in the best way, either in terms of their own vocation and training, or in terms of a satisfactory understanding of the priest's work. The anonymous contributor of the Preface to *Crockford's Clerical Directory, 1980-82* has observed that increasing ecumenical agreement about the nature of the priesthood has not been accompanied by a similar clarification of what the job entails. The writer refers to 'a crisis of confidence in the hearts of many ordained ministers, who work hard but are not sure that it is work which they ought to be doing'. The conclusion drawn from this situation is that 'the time has come for radical thoughts and experiments'.[3]

EIGHT POSSIBLE ROLES

163.   The crisis has not developed without a great deal of thinking (some of it radical, some not) about the problem of the priest's role in the contemporary Church. One or more of eight categories are suggested as being definitive.

### (1) The Priest as Leader

Our inherited expectations of having one beneficed clergyman to each parish, possibly with junior assistants, has naturally emphasised the leadership role of the clergy. They are the ones who take initiatives, make or control policy decisions, and determine the agenda of the local Church. Giving 'sole charge' of a parish to one man effectively settles the question of leadership. This pattern of deployment has in turn affected the Church's selection procedures for its clergy, since it is potential incumbents who are required. Now the development of lay ministry has actually enhanced this leadership role. In secular terms the parish priest is regarded as the 'branch manager' of a service industry. Some of the clergy, especially those who have been employed in managerial positions prior to their ordination, fit into this administrative and organisational role very easily and the lay officers of the Church discover that they relate to them very well. It will be argued in Chapter 15, however, that the local Church should produce its own leadership, and that different kinds of leadership are required for different purposes. A corporate leadership of the local Church is to be preferred to the comings and goings of individual clergy, each with their own prescription for the renewal of the Church.

### (2) The Priest as Pastor

It can hardly be denied that a priest is supposed to be pastoring somebody. The question is, who? The cure of all souls within the parish has become an impossible undertaking unless the charge in the Ordinal of the *Book of Common Prayer* 'to seek for Christ's sheep that are dispersed abroad' is transmuted into a policy of keeping open all hours for any returning wanderers. Besides, the Church's pastors have now been matched in their professional concern by other caring agencies in the community. Among the faithful and enquirers there may be plenty of pastoral work to be done, but again it will be argued in Chapter 15 that to channel this work of pastoring through one minister is to set inevitable limits to church growth, and to restrict the scope of ministry to the range of one person's abilities and experience. A shared pastorate including lay ministers should be sought for each congregation. The *Crockford's* Preface-writer already referred to also pointed out 'that the idea that a fully professional ministry can be or ought to be chiefly responsible for the pastoral care of all the parishes in England is not two centuries old'.[4]

### (3) The Priest as a Focus of Community

The priest by his commitment to the Gospel is able to identify in his own person the Christian community. He represents the commitment of the whole community, and when he presides at the Eucharist (or, as some would express, it 'offers the sacrifice') he represents Christ within the community. This is a symbolic role; it is also a kind of leadership. The trouble is that the more places there are in which he is required to enact this symbolic role the less effective he is as a focus of community. A priest who travels round a number of churches on Sunday is in danger of denying the very sign he is meant to be. Residence, familiarity, acceptance and trust would appear to be desirable features of such a ministry. Certainly a priest is a sign of the catholic Church, as his ordination and appointment by the Bishop clearly demonstrate, but his presence identifies a particular congregation as the *local manifestation* of the catholic Church, not as some lesser kind of Christian community. It is therefore most appropriate for the local Church to put forward one or more from among their own number to fulfil this ministry. Not every congregation will be in a position to do this. A local priest must have qualities of personal and spiritual maturity. Those chosen must respond with an inward sense of divine calling. The sign of Christian community should be a witness beyond the congregation, but it is easy for an individual to be identified, not with the community as a whole, but with one class or section within it. A particular problem at present may be that in some places the person most suitable for this role is ineligible by reason of her sex. Despite these difficulties it is important for the effectiveness of a future strategy that local Churches are invited to identify, from among their pastoral leadership, those who may be called to a local priesthood.

### (4) The Priest as Public Spokesman

The priest is a representative minister in the further sense that he is regarded by society as an official spokeman for the Church. He embodies the institution he represents. This is a rather different matter from the lay apostolate of taking Christ into the world and representing him in ministering to one another. An individual Christian may adopt a more or less critical stance towards the Church as an institution, but the priest takes public responsibility for it. There are situations in which this ministry is highly important: it will take one form where a church building and its services fulfil a civic role; it will appear differently where the clergy occupy positions of responsibility in the community; it is an important element in some specialist ministries; it is a factor which needs to be weighed by many entering the non-stipendiary ministry. Although this is an inescapable element in the ordained ministry of the Church of England, and a major aspect of the work of some priests, it could hardly be described as the heart of a priest's vocation. It will be accomplished best by those who gain least fulfilment from it, and most disastrously by those who manage to project either a bureaucratic or a hierarchical image.

### (5) The Priest as Guardian of the Tradition

The ARCIC Statement on 'Ministry and Ordination' attributes to the ordained ministry responsibility for 'fidelity to the apostolic faith, its embodiment in the life of the Church today, and its transmission to the Church of tomorrow'.[5] In his book on *Ministry–A Case for Change*, the Dutch Dominican scholar Edward Schillebeeckx refers to the Church's foundation upon the ministry of the apostles. In his view the essential task of the ordained ministry is to maintain the Church in its apostolicity.[6] The teaching office of the priesthood is therefore undoubtedly of the greatest significance. Yet a number of adjustments need to be made to any picture of clerical sermonising from pulpits 'six feet above contradiction'. Three may be referred to in passing. One is that a guardian of something of great value neither owns it nor monopolises it; indeed, the word guardian is inadequate if it suggests that the clergy possess the key of theological knowledge. Theology belongs to the laity. Second, the word guardian is further inadequate if it suggests the curator of a museum. A true stewardship of the treasure of God's Word requires an openness to critical questioning and a capacity to reflect on how the contemporary context establishes it as living truth. Third, the teaching of the faith 'once delivered to the saints' is but one part of the ministry of the Word. The Church is 'built upon the foundation laid by the apostles and *prophets*, and Christ Jesus himself is the foundation stone' (Ephesians 2.20 NEB). Robin Gill has explored some of the difficulties of combining priestly with prophetic ministry, yet it is widely assumed today that priests are supposed to be prophets.[7] In fact the identification of the priest with the institution, mentioned in the last paragraph, limits the possibilities of prophetic witness, although as a faithful servant of God the priest is called to minister the Word to the Church without fear or favour.

### (6) The Priest as a Professional Minister

People rightly expect a certain professionalism from the clergy in the sense of their having an expertise in their field. But what is their field? All Christians must surely be professionals in the basic meaning of the word: to make public confession of one's faith. Is there a more particular skill or learning which belongs to the ordained ministry? The answer depends upon whether we mean this in an exclusive sense. Doctors are not the only people who have made a study of medicine, and lawyers are not the only ones who possess a knowledge of the law. What these professionals have secured is an exclusive right to practise their skills on behalf of others. Within the Church the Bishops control who is authorised to perform a ministry of Word and Sacraments. But there is here a crucial difference from other professionals. Although certain formal acts are restricted to those in orders, the substance of a ministry of Word and Sacraments, that is to say the application of skill and learning for this purpose, is by no means restricted to the clergy. Indeed it is freely practised all the time within the charismatic life of the Christian community. Furthermore the ministry of readers shows that the Bishop's licence to preach is not at present restricted to those who are in orders. If we use the word professional to indicate those who have been authorised to undertake a particular ministry then the Church's professional ministers are at present a wider body than the clergy alone.

*(7) The Priest as Enabler of the Laity*

Ever since the ministry of the laity began to receive encouragement in the Church of England a re-interpretation of the distinctive role of the clergy has been necessary, and the one most often expressed is that the task of the clergy is to enable the laity to fulfil their ministry. However true and appropriate this may be, it is not particularly distinctive. The clergy endeavour to be enablers of the laity; the laity are certainly enablers of the clergy, and there is on reflection no such thing as a ministry which is *not* enabling to others. Nor does the concept assist the clergy in determining their priorities. Teaching and pastoral care are enabling ministries, but so essentially is administration. It is also misleading to regard the work of the clergy as limited to the congregation, and so enabling the ministry of the laity in the world. Although there are particular responsibilities for Christian nurture which have been given to the ordained ministry, the whole life and work of the priest must be committed to mission.

*(8) The Priest as Church-builder*

A final view of the ordained ministry sees it as having a kind of sliding scale of significance in proportion to the strength or weakness of the Church in each place. The priest's role is most important, not where the size of the congregation is an impressive witness to his success, but where the flock of Christ has not been gathered. Where the laity, through the evangelistic, teaching and pastoral work of the clergy, have grown to spiritual maturity the need for ordained ministry declines, until in heaven there will be no orders at all, just the one royal priesthood of the people of God.

RESULTS OF THIS ANALYSIS

164.   The picture which results from the eight roles of the priesthood just enumerated is a confusing one. It indicates plenty for the priest to do, but what is his essential task? It is not possible to build a clear job description for the work of a priest which will apply to all. Attempts to write one are in fact

bound to fail. I have seen a vocational leaflet entitled *Wanted: Leaders in Tomorrow's Church.* It contains a quite excellent summary of the qualifications and personal qualities required in the Church's ordained ministers. When it proceeds to describe their work, however, its effect can only be to discourage all except the foolish and the conceited:

'He will be a leader of the church's worship and a man of prayer, whose oversight encourages others to discover and exercise their vocation and gifts.

'He will be a planner and thinker, who communicates a vision of future goals and who seeks with others to achieve them.

'He will be a pastor and spiritual director, who is skilled in understanding, counselling, supporting and reconciling both groups and individuals.

'He will be a prophet, evangelist and teacher, who proclaims and witnesses to the Gospel, and who makes available today the riches of the church's tradition and experience.

'He will be an administrator and co-ordinator, with responsibility for the Christian management and organisation of the local church's resources.'

Since this leaflet was compiled by a group of parochial clergy, it presumably sets out what they were themselves aiming to do—and who would deny that it is what many Church members still think that their clergy should be doing?

165.  There is little point in writing job descriptions of this sort (either deliberately or unconsciously) because there are few people with the necessary gifts to fill them. An important objective of a future strategy must be to end the 'general practitioner' role of the clergy which is at present normally expected in the parochial ministry. Every servant of God is called to a specialist ministry—the one which employs effectively that person's particular gifts. It is quite clear that within the ordained ministry there is a great diversity of gifts; no checklist can be compiled of those which are essential. The passage from the leaflet just quoted amounts to a fine summary of the ministry which is needed in each local Church, but what possible advantage is there in attempting to provide all this through one individual?

166.  One conclusion is evident for clergy appointments: *in each case a job description relating to that particular post should be drawn up,* so that it is clear what sort of gifts are needed in the minister to be appointed.

DIOCESAN AND LOCAL PRIESTS

167.  In addition to the existence of a wide variety of gifts within the priesthood it is possible to discern in the ordained ministry of the Church of England a combination of two traditions. The Rt Revd John Taylor, Bishop of Winchester, described these in November 1980 in a speech to the General Synod:

'There is the tradition of a local parochial community, with a fully sacramental congregation served by its own ordained minister as one focal point of its identity, and there is the tradition of a fully professional clergy, professional as

101

to the standard of their specialist training, professional as to the parity of their common discourse.'[8]

The professional standards of the clergy, applied nationally both in their selection and their training, permit them to be deployed in furtherance of the Church's mission. The local Church needs a focal point of its identity resident in the parochial community. We have here elements of two traditions in the ordained ministry which are in fact much more ancient than Anglicanism. They are referred to in the commentary on the WCC Lima text:

'The earliest Church knew both the travelling ministry of such missionaries as Paul and the local ministry of leadership in places where the Gospel was received.'[9]

168.   The modern presbyterate in the Church of England incorporates both of these elements, for good reasons which have to do with the association of the presbyterate with the episcopate in carrying out the Bishop's apostolic and pastoral functions. However, there is a sense in which the manner of doing this in the Church of England has become detrimental to both evangelistic and pastoral ministry. It is not proposed that the one universal priesthood should be divided into two, but that its members should be more clearly appointed either to a local or to a wider ministry by a distinction being made between local and diocesan priests. If it is objected that this would result in a two-level priesthood it is suggested in reply that such a distinction is truer to the historic realities of the ordained ministry than are those other distinctions which are spreading at present between stipendiary and non-stipendiary, full-time and part-time, parochial and specialist clergy. Local priests would be called from within the pastoral leadership of each local Church. Diocesan priests would be called into association with the Bishop in carrying out his responsibility to provide ministry where the local Church was lacking in necessary resources. Many would therefore be working in parochial ministry, others in what would at present be termed specialist posts. Wherever they served, two conditions would apply to all diocesan priests. The first is that they would not be engaged in 'general duties' but would be fulfilling a ministry in accordance with their particular gifts. The second is that every one would be a member of a diocesan ministry team. Some of these teams would assist the local Church in parishes and cells through secondment to deanery mission committees. Other teams would work throughout the diocese in the way that education teams currently operate. Local priests would be undertaking a voluntary role within the fellowship of the local Church and this will receive further attention in Chapter 15. Diocesan priests would include both maintained (i.e. stipendiary) ministers and non-stipendiary priest-workers.

169.   The differing emphases envisaged in the respective ministries of diocesan and local priests may be summarised as follows:

*i) The primary concerns of diocesan priests would be missionary and educational:*

> evangelistic work;
> community involvement;
> preaching and teaching the faith;
> counselling and spiritual direction;
> conducting retreats and leading prayer groups;
> involvement with training courses;
> consultative contributions to local churches.

*ii) The primary concerns of local priests would be pastoral and administrative:*

> leadership in the local Church;
> provision and development of teaching and pastoral care,
>     worship, sacraments and discipline in the local Church;
> identification of objectives and organisation of programmes
>     for the local Church;
> administration of church affairs;
> co-ordination with other local churches in the deanery.

*iii) All priests, diocesan and local, would be concerned*

> to undertake a ministry of prayer;
> to enable the ministry of the laity in the world;
> to act as representative persons on behalf of the Church and as
>     focal points of ministry within the life of the Church.

PROPOSALS FOR THE EXISTING NON-STIPENDIARY PRIESTHOOD

170.   The 1983 ACCM Report on the Non-Stipendiary Ministry has revealed the diverse character of this development in the Church's ordained ministry. Originally the Bishops' Regulations for NSM distinguished between a retirement ministry which was virtually full-time but unpaid, and the ordination of men who remained in secular employment. By the end of the seventies it had become clear that the latter category included some whose sphere of ministry was firmly based in a parish, some who had opportunities for a pastoral ministry to individuals in their places of work, and some who could see their whole occupation in priestly terms. When proposals for a specifically local ordained ministry were considered by the House of Bishops in 1979 it was decided that this should be regarded as one more variation within the general category of non-stipendiary ministry. At present, therefore, NSM is a title covering a range of ordained ministry which has little in common beyond the fact that it is performed without the assistance of a stipend.

171.   Most NSMs are devoted to parochial ministry and do as much in the parish as time allows. Some experience frustration at not being able to do

more, and this must be a factor influencing the high proportion of younger non-stipendiary priests who transfer to stipendiary ministry. In terms of this strategy, persons with gifts and concern for the mission of their own local Church would be candidates for a local priesthood. They would thus be recognised and authorised for the actual ministry which they felt called to undertake. The local priesthood would not be some sort of inferior class of clergy: it would reflect the needs and resources for ministry of each locality. A wide variety of persons would become local priests because their ministry would have to be related to the particular community in which it was exercised. In each case, however, the sphere of ministry would be totally clear. A move to another locality would mean that a local priest might not be able to begin what would be a new local ministry immediately. The NSM Report reveals, however, that despite general mobility in the population only 10% of NSMs have so far moved diocese since ordination.

172.    The vast majority of existing NSMs are drawn from the ranks of teachers and other professional groups, managers, administrators, and other non-manual workers. This may simply reflect the preponderance of these groups among the Church's male employed membership as a whole. It does, however, convey a rather limited vision of the possibilities for priest-workers, and it appears that relatively few NSMs have found the main centre of their ministry at work despite attention given to this dimension during training and some notable attempts to develop an adequate theology for priests ministering in and through their secular occupations.[10] The missionary dimension to the work of diocesan priests in this strategy readily includes the contribution of those with a calling to minister through their positions in industry, commerce, education, medicine and government. There are, however, four important qualifications which need to be kept in view:

    i) A vocation to the priesthood involves a readiness by the candidate, if it seems good to the Lord and to the Church, to leave an existing occupation.

    ii) It is valid for some priests, while not seeing themselves as in any sense part-time, to regard their jobs as primarily a means of livelihood rather than their sphere of ministry. This was presumably the reason for Paul's tent-making.

    iii) All priest-workers should be members of diocesan ministry teams, and moreover be related to a Christian cell including other people from their place of work.

    iv) While he is ordained to ministry as a priest in the Church of God, it is a fact that not all the Christian colleagues of an Anglican priest-worker will recognise his representative office. There is therefore a limitation on his priesthood even at this level; claims that a priest-worker acts as a priest of mankind or even of creation are complete distortions of the significance of the Order of Priests within the Church.

173.   The NSM Report has found that there is a limit to how far NSMs can be deployed and contribute to any overall diocesan strategy. Yet it is reasonable to ask whether the Church actually needs to deploy an NSM as a priest in a particular place and within the terms and conditions of his existing secular employment. A specialist stipendiary priest may be engaged there already. For example, it has been known for university lecturers to offer as NSMs because they felt they could do a better job than the existing chaplains! On the other hand, as the NSM Report notes, there are openings for non-stipendiary ministry in places of higher education which are completely complementary to the work of the full-time chaplains. In places of work where a lay Christian witness is established without a stipendiary priest being available it may be appropriate for an NSM candidate to be put forward from the group, just as a parish might put forward someone for local priesthood. NSM priests with particular gifts might be deployed in a ministry over a wide area of a diocese, or in a particular diocesan project.

NUMBER OF DIOCESAN PRIESTS REQUIRED

174.   It will become apparent from the strategy for the local Church to be developed in Chapter 15 that ideally each parochial congregation would have a leadership team or eldership including at least one voluntary local priest. In practice there would undoubtedly be at any one time many congregations unable to achieve this. Their need of ordained ministry would have to be met by diocesan priests. In addition, the increasing opportunities for specialist posts in secular institutions and the widespread need of 'specialist' resources among local Churches ensure that diocesan bishops would continue to have work for as many priests as they could obtain. The planned disappearance of a general parochial ministry is no ground for a reduction in numbers of full-time ministers. This is a strategy, not for making do with fewer clergy, but for making the most effective use of the ministry of as many as are available. There are two conceivable limits only to the size of the stipendiary priesthood: the number who are truly called and the number who can be adequately maintained. In respect of these limits there are two observations to be noted:

   i) The call of God is to the priesthood, not to the stipendiary priesthood: therefore all whose gifts and calling are recognised by the Church should be ordained, but it should be accepted that payment of a stipend is not essential to the fulfilment of a priest's vocation.

   ii) At all times the Church has maintained as much ministry as it could possibly afford, knowing that its mission will be assisted by freeing gifted and dedicated servants of God for ministry wherever and in whatever way the Spirit may direct.

175.   In this chapter we have accepted much of what is currently understood by ordained ministry as valid priestly work, but have called for clear job descriptions to indicate which aspects of this ministry are relevant to particular posts. We return now to the question of what is fundamental to the priesthood, and the definition put forward is neither ontological nor functional, but in terms of the relationship between ministries. It was argued in Chapter 11 that all Christians have a ministry through the recognition and exercise of their distinctive gifts. It is the purpose of Orders to relate the local Church to the wider Church, and for this purpose the Bishop is the focus of the Church's unity. Through association with his ministry the college of presbyters, including both diocesan and local priests, helps to fulfil his responsibility by supplying the needs of local Churches. At the same time the president of each local eucharistic community, whether a local or a diocesan priest, by his association with the Bishop, maintains the local Church in fellowship with him, and through him with the universal Church.

NOTES TO CHAPTER 13: THE PRIESTS

[1]A. Russell, *The Clerical Profession*, SPCK, 1980, esp. pp.233–88. Dr Russell notes, e.g., that 'whereas other professional men have come to terms with the idea that, in an advanced society, they must necessarily be employed within bureaucratic structures, the clergy have consistently indicated that they are unwilling to change in this way, despite the inadequacies of the present system' (p.271).

[2]P. Coleman, 'Prospects for the professional ministry', editorial in *Theology*, Nov. 1982, p.402.

[3]*Crockford's Clerical Directory 1980-82*, Oxford University Press, 1983, p.xxii.

[4]*Ibid.*, p.xxiii.

[5]ARCIC, *The Final Report*, p.33, para.9.

[6]E. Schillebeeckx, *Ministry–A Case for Change*, SCM Press, ET 1981, esp. pp.33–7.

[7]R. Gill, *Prophecy and Praxis: The Social Function of the Churches*, Marshall, Morgan and Scott, 1981, esp. pp.59–75, 128–136.

[8]*General Synod Report of Proceedings*, vol.11, no.3, November Group of Sessions 1980, p.922.

[9]*BEM*, p.25, Commentary on para.21.

[10]See e.g. M. Bourke, 'The Theology of a Non-Stipendiary Ministry' in *Theology*, May 1981, pp.177–82; and M. Ranken, 'A Theology for the Priest at Work', in *Theology*, March 1982, pp.108–13.

# 14: The Deacons

176.   The other Order which is associated with the Bishop in the provision of ministry in the diocese is the Diaconate. At present few members of the Church of England are conscious of the presence of deacons among them in any other form than as very new assistant curates in parishes, who are still too inexperienced to undertake the full duties of priestly ministry without further training on the job. In due course, that is to say after a year or two at the most, unless some reason for delay has become apparent in the meantime, deacons become 'fully-fledged' priests. Deacons are therefore regarded as being either trainee, or, if they continue for long as such, somehow defective or sub-standard priests. Theologically it is accepted that priests and bishops do not cease to be deacons when they are ordained and consecrated: they fulfil their ministry in a diaconal way, namely, by serving others. But there has been no clear and positive reason for remaining a deacon and in practice very few have done so. It has failed to remain a ministry in its own right to which it is usual for individuals to be called; it has become a rung on a hierarchical ladder.

177.   This situation will change somewhat if the legislation which is now in preparation for the admission of women to the Order of Deacon receives the approval of the General Synod. There will then of necessity be a 'permanent' diaconate in the Church of England, because some members of it will not be eligible to move on to the priesthood. The anomalous position of deaconesses will be improved by the inclusion within the diaconate of an Order of women which clearly already denotes a diaconal ministry. But the result will hardly do justice to a 'distinctive' diaconate, unless significant numbers of both men and women respond to a call to fulfil their vocation by remaining within the diaconate rather than seeking the priesthood. It is fair to suppose that they are unlikely to do this unless the Church clarifies its thinking about the purpose of the diaconate, and therefore knows who should be recognised as called to this ministry.

178.   With this in mind, in July 1981 the General Synod of the Church of England passed the following private member's motion:

> 'That this Synod requests the House of Bishops to consider ways in which the Diaconate can once more become a vital and active element in the threefold Ministry in the Church of England, and bring to this Synod practical proposals. In particular consideration of the following possibilities is requested:

i) That it should be a ministry open to men and women on a lifelong basis, in addition to its present use as a probationary period before Ordination to the Priesthood;

ii) Any proposals brought forward should not be in a form which in any way prejudges questions relating to the Ordination of Women to the Priesthood;

iii) That selection for this Ministry, and training for it, need not be in the same form as that adopted for the Priesthood.'

The Church thus possesses an Order of ministry which it recognises at present lacks a distinctive role. In the past it has considered abolishing it or leaving it as it is.[1] It has now resolved that this ministry should if possible be revitalised. What might such a revived diaconate look like?

### THE EXPERIENCE OF OTHER CHURCHES

179.   Diaconal ministry is inevitably present in all Churches, since it is the way of Christ himself. A glance at the various expressions of it in different Churches quickly confirms, however, that there is no clear form for the diaconate which is common to them all. *Diakonia*, The World Federation of Diaconal Associations and Sisterhoods, which is due to hold its fourteenth international assembly in Britain in the summer of 1983, is itself an illustration of this diversity worldwide. In Britain, the Churches' Council for Covenanting recognised the same feature:

'The forms in which the Churches have preserved the diaconal ministry are perhaps more varied than for any other order . . . The Council has found it very difficult to provide a succinct description of the ministry of deacons that does full justice to the range of the Churches' contemporary experience.'[2]

There are no deacons in the United Reformed Church. In the Baptist Churches in this country they are not ordained, but carry out administrative and pastoral duties as office-holders rather than on the basis of a lifelong vocation. The Methodist Church ceased admitting women to the Wesley Deaconess Order in 1979. A document entitled *The Development of Ministries* was presented to the Methodist Conference in 1982, which proposed 'a single order of lay ministers' containing 'a considerable variety of forms of ministry' and including the remaining Wesley Deaconesses. However, a further report to be presented to the Conference in 1983 and entitled *The Diaconate and other Authorised Lay Ministries* notes 'the absence of an ecumenical consensus with regard to a diaconate', and proposes an order of about 50 full-time deacons with 'an emphasis on teaching and pastoral ministries' and in addition the recognition of other authorised lay ministries.[3] The WCC Lima text has suggested that 'the threefold ministry of bishop, presbyter and deacon may serve today as an expression of the unity we seek and also as a means for achieving it'.[4]

180.   Since the Second Vatican Council the Roman Catholic Church has addressed itself to the position of deacons. The Constitution on the Church

*(Lumen Gentium)* spoke of the need for the diaconate to be 'restored as a proper and permanent rank of the hierarchy'. In 1967 were published 'General Norms for Restoring the Permanent Diaconate in the Latin Church', which stated that the diaconate 'is not to be considered as a mere step towards the priesthood', but as a 'permanent' vocation. Although it remains a 'lower grade' of the hierarchy it is not on that account to be used merely as a staging-post. In practice the development of the permanent diaconate in the Roman Catholic Church has inevitably reflected the fact that it has been opened to married men, whereas the priesthood remains celibate. By this means a pastoral and liturgical ministry is provided in priestless parishes by people who are not qualified to proceed to the priesthood.

181.  Within the Anglican Communion a permanent diaconate is being developed in some places where the priesthood does include not only married men, but women as well. An example is the Episcopal Church in the USA. It is interesting to note, however, that the House of Bishops of that Church meeting in 1979 to consider a report, *The Church, the Diaconate, the Future*, 'noted the great diversity of both theology and practice which was emerging and felt further study and monitoring was justified. They asked for a three year study . . . but soon extended it into a six year study with pilot dioceses who are to report quite fully at the 1985 Convention.'[5] There is clearly a common urge among the Churches to explore what the diaconate could mean today, but as yet no ready-made form in existence elsewhere which could be adopted by the Church of England.

TWO INAPPROPRIATE DEVELOPMENTS

182.  Besides the useful indications of development in diaconal ministry which do exist, and from which the Church of England can certainly learn, there are also some tendencies which it would be quite inappropriate for us to follow. Two of the latter will be examined.

*(1) Deacons as Pastors of the Local Church*

At an ecumenical conference on the diaconate held in London a Roman Catholic deacon acknowledged that shortage of priests was making it difficult to establish the norm of a permanent diaconate in his own Church. Deacons are easily regarded as fillers of a priestly vacuum, and this confusion is made all the more likely because much of what any parish priest does during any week is diaconal so there are spheres of overlap between priest and deacon.[6] A similar problem has been identified by the Roman Catholic Church in Belgium:

> 'As soon as he is ordained, all or almost all of the deacon's activity consists of help of various kinds to the clergy (baptism, liturgy, marriages, funerals, communion of the sick). This help is useful and fruitful: it answers daily needs. But does it contribute to the renewal of ordained ministries?'[7]

109

The lesson seems clear for the Church of England's own strategy: deacons could easily become what readers have all too often been, a clerical-substitute ministry lacking a distinctive contribution of their own. In seeking vocations to the diaconate the Church should not be looking for gifted lay people who could help the vicar with pastoral work and take services in his absence. It is true that it would be very desirable to have a properly accredited form of local ministry which avoided the unrealistic expectations which are bound to be laid upon local priests. It is doubtful, however, whether deacons *in the absence of priests* ever could successfully avoid those expectations; and their existence would not solve one major problem at least which is created by a shortage of priests, namely, the presidency of the Eucharist. Deacons have not generally been, and in terms of this strategy should not become, pastors of local churches. A different approach to local ministry will be advocated in this report.

*(2) The Diaconate as a Lay Order*

An opposite tendency is to regard the diaconate as a lay order of ministry, which would somehow escape those aspects of clericalisation which set the priesthood apart from the laity in ways which are constantly threatening to de-skill rather than to enable the faithful. Put like this it sounds rather like an attempt to abandon the priesthood as a lost cause and begin again. The better policy is clearly to develop a truly enabling priesthood. So far from a lay diaconate releasing the ministry of the laity, it is highly likely to appear as the invention of a truly clerically-minded Church. We have already argued that the Church has Orders, and it has gifts for ministry. Orders exist to serve and to represent the whole laity, whereas the separate ministries within the laity are expressed by the due recognition of gifts. It is therefore confusing to propose an 'omnium gatherum' of lay ministry as the basis for a revived diaconate. At one and the same time this would suggest that the other Orders do not also represent the whole laity, and prevent within the laity a proper distinction in the recognition of gifts by suggesting that the creation of an order is necessary to undertake ministry which is at present being carried out perfectly adequately by lay people. Worst of all would be the notion that something revolutionary could be achieved by reserving certain functions in the liturgy to a group of people suitably attired and set apart as deacons. The idea of a 'de-clericalised' order is attractive, and one to be pursued; but there is no transparent reason why a revived diaconate is more likely to avoid the snares of clerisy than the existing episcopate, priesthood or, for that matter, readers. The prospects are already somewhat clouded by the fact that at present trainee priests adopt all the clerical trappings at the point of their admission to the diaconate. (There is a question as to how the public ministry of deacons is to be identified; but any distinctive symbol or dress should surely be different from that adopted by priests.) In any case it is unnecessary here to pursue the chimera of a lay diaconate: the resolution of the General Synod calls for a restoration of the diaconate as 'a vital and

110

active element in the threefold Ministry in the Church of England'. It is therefore as one of the historic Orders that it is to be considered.

THE BISHOP AND HIS DEACONS

183.  Among all the uncertainties about the origin and function of deacons in the early Church there is one feature which appears to be constantly maintained, and that is the relationship between bishops and deacons. It is true that a clear picture of this is not available in the New Testament, unless one discerns an anticipation of it in the appointment of the Seven as assistants to the Twelve in Acts 6. On the other hand there is nothing to suggest a different line of development. In the early third century the *Apostolic Tradition* states that the deacon 'is not ordained for the priesthood, but for serving the bishop'; and the canons of Nicea in 325 stipulate: 'Let the deacons keep within their proper bounds, knowing that they are the ministers of the bishop.' It is interesting to note from Eusebius that during the time of Bishop Cornelius (*c.*251–3) the church in Rome had forty-six presbyters but only seven deacons. There is no suggestion that at this stage they were trainee priests; they were assistants to the Bishop. In an un-published thesis Tom Dye has summarised the evidence as follows:

'It would appear that, from an early date, the Deacons were seen as the assistants of the Leaders of the Church in the care of the sick and needy, and the administration of the Eucharist. When the Mono-episcopate emerged they became the Bishop's assistants in this task.'[8]

184.  Putting the historic nature of the diaconate together with the theo-logical understanding of orders developed in a previous section it is possible to see the deacon as representing the whole serving Church and enabling the serving ministry of the whole Church, and doing both by association with the Bishop in his diocese. The diaconal character of many ministries is evident, from visiting the sick to serving coffee after the Sunday Eucharist; indeed, the example of Christ indicates that there must be a diaconal approach to all ministry. There are no traditional functions of a deacon which may not be undertaken by lay people. But the Order of Deacons is part of the Bishop's provision of ministry in his diocese; that is what it expresses: it does not monopolise any ministerial function. It would be natural to expect that most existing licensed ministers other than priests would want to be admitted to such a revived diaconate (e.g. deaconesses, lay workers, Church Army officers, social workers). The exception would be that some of these might see their ministry as essentially one which is called forth by the local Church for leadership in that community. Their position is one which will be con-sidered later. Although it might appear that the Church's 'professional' and accredited lay ministry has thus after all been gathered into one lay order, the point must be re-emphasised that deacons are not a lay ministry; by association with the Bishop they are an Order, representative of the whole laity.

111

185. Some existing accredited lay ministers may protest that they would thus lose their lay status. Such an attitude would either be an anachronism in the de-clericalised Church here envisaged, or else suggest that those who feel this way should be undertaking a truly lay ministry, that is one which does not require any authorisation from the Bishop beyond their baptism. The diaconate, like the priesthood, would be an order containing many gifts for ministry. It could therefore include the theologian, the administrator, the healer, and the evangelist. Like the diocesan priests in maintained and sector ministries the deacons would be available for the mission of the Church and to enable the ministry of the laity, as directed by the Bishop.

THE WORK OF DEACONS

186. There are many reasons why the Church needs, and needs to maintain in ministry, a supply of deacons as well as priests. First of all there will always be those who are called to devote themselves to 'caring for the poor, the needy, the sick, and all who are in trouble'.[9] They will be found particularly in hospitals, in prisons, in city centres and in the depressed parts of our cities; in old people's welfare, in rehabilitation centres, in projects for the young and the unemployed. Deacons are ordained as a focus of the Church's diaconal ministry, which is the call of God to serve the world in Christ's name. Perhaps the most essential vision, therefore, is to see the role of the deacon as a community servant. Diaconal ministry would not be so tied conceptually to the parochial context as is true generally of the presbyterate. *Diakonia* has always been expressed through the active involvement of the Church in service to the secular community in a wide variety of ways. Dean Edward Patey, in a report of an ecumenical encounter on 'Koinonia and Diakonia' held at L'Arbresle, France in 1976, points out that the nineteenth century in this country saw a great revival of diaconal ministry through Christian inspired social service organisations and institutions (e.g. Barnardo's, the Church of England Children's Society, etc.). More recent developments such as the Samaritans, Shelter, etc., are also seen by many Christians as a logical development of the Church's diaconal ministry, even though such organisations may have few or no institutional links with ecclesiastical structures. Perhaps the State itself has been helped to find a diaconal vocation. Meanwhile local congregations have been experiencing a renewal of Christian community life ('koinonia'). Dean Patey adds:

> 'This is beginning to raise acutely the question of the relationship between the Church as community, and the mission of the Church to the secular community in which it is set.'[19]

The ministry of deacons is at the very centre of this relationship. There may be a number of men who have been ordained as non-stipendiary priest-workers in recent years, the nature of whose witness is not priestly but diaconal within the secular community. No less than the priest-worker, however, the deacon as community servant needs to be operating firmly within the context of the witness of the whole Church, and one Christian community in particular. Often the opportunities for ministry will be specifically parochial. There should not be any separation of the Church's liturgical ministry from its public service. The 1968 Lambeth Conference spoke of the diaconate as a distinctive ministry 'combining service of others with liturgical functions' (Resolution 32). It is true that this could describe the ministry of any Christian, but that is not the point. To quote Dean Patey again:

> 'Those who are ordained to a diaconal ministry have (a particular) task of showing the inextricable link between diakonia and proclamation, and between diakonia and worship.'[11]

WHO IS CALLED?

187.   That brings us to the heart of the problem of diaconal ministry, which is that the concept can become simply too generalised. 'Deacon' is one of the frequent New Testament words for minister. All Christian ministry is to be understood in terms of service, and sacrificial service at that (Mark 10.45). All followers of Christ are called to be deacons, as servants of God, of their fellow-Christians, and of all humanity. Just as there is a priesthood of all believers, so there is a diaconate of all believers. Just as the Order of Priests can therefore be a sign to the whole Church of its priestly ministry, so the Order of Deacons can be a sign of the whole serving Church. Others in the congregation may perform diaconal functions, but the deacon is a constant reminder of the fundamental character of Christ's own ministry (Luke 22.27). For that reason it is appropriate for the Church's bishops and priests to come to their ministry through admission to the diaconate. No-one can say he is not called to it. The difficulty is to avoid the conclusion that either every baptised Christian should be made a deacon, or else the experience should be confined to those who are called to the priesthood, as a necessary preliminary response.

188.   These two alternatives obscure what might be the distinctive role of an Order of Deacons. I believe that the sign of the whole Church's *diakonia* will be most effectively established if there is in association with the Bishops an Order of Deacons standing alongside the Order of Priests which is equally demanding in terms of the selection, training, and potentially life-long commitment required of its members. The personal and spiritual criteria employed in selection would be the same. Diaconal formation should not be done 'on the cheap'; standards required would be comparable, though not necessarily identical, to those for the priesthood. This is examined in greater detail in Chapters 18 and 19. In particular, a fully professional training should be required in those specialist areas in which individual deacons may be working. Deacons, no less than priests, will be set apart for public ministry on behalf of the whole Church. They must know what they are about.

189. What they *are* about, in all things, is a true service to humanity. That is not the same thing as saying that the Church needs in the diaconate volunteers who are keen to 'help people'. The ministry of the Gospel is not just an ambulance service. The diaconate of Jesus included washing his friends' feet; it also included turning merchants out of the Temple. It involved him in relieving physical hunger, but also in rebuking lack of spiritual hunger. His absolute insistence on the priority of God's claims, and his direct speech to those who had made a mess of their own lives and the lives of others, revealed unfailingly the One whose will he served in all things. In its *diakonia* the Church must find a call to ministries of evangelism, of prophecy, of discernment and of prayer; ministries offered in a spirit of service without power by those who are glad to be servants for Christ's sake.

## NOTES TO CHAPTER 14: THE DEACONS

[1]Cf. *Deacons in the Church:* The Report of a Working Party set up by the Advisory Council for the Church's Ministry, 1974; and *The Ministry of Deacons and Deaconesses:* A Report by the Advisory Council for the Church's Ministry, GS 344, 1977.

[2]*Towards Visible Unity: Proposals for a Covenant:* The Report of the Churches' Council for Covenanting, 1980, p.53.

[3]*The Development of Ministries:* A Report of the Division of Ministries of the Methodist Church; *The Diaconate and Other Authorised Lay Ministries.*

[4]*BEM*, p.24, para.22.

[5]Sister Teresa, Dss. CSA, *An Exploration of the Diaconate in the Episcopal Church (USA)*, Distinctive Diaconate Studies, 27, 1982, p.2.

[6]See R. Searls, *Journal of the Consultative Conference on the Permanent Diaconate (Ecumenically Considered)*, Distinctive Diaconate Studies, 16, 1981, p.2.

[7]A. Geerts, quoted in *Pro Mundi Vita*, April 1980, p.7.

[8]T. L. Dye, 'The Theology of the Self-Supporting Ministry', M.Phil. thesis, University of Hull, 1976, p.143.

[9]The Ordination of Deacons, *The Alternative Service Book 1980*, p.344.

[10]*Koinonia–Diakonia: In search of a relevant community.* An Ecumenical Encounter held at the Centre St Dominique, L'Arbresle, France, 1976, p.3.

[11]*Ibid.*, p.7.

# 15: Leadership in the Local Church

OVERSIGHT (EPISCOPE) IN THE CHURCH
190.   It has already been stated that a crucial response in making a future strategy effective will be the acceptance by the local Church of its responsibility to undertake the mission of the Church in that particular place. It must be prepared to see itself not just as a part of the one Catholic Church, but as *the* local manifestation of the Catholic Church. It *is* the Body of Christ, and therefore it contains within itself potential for ministry, and has laid upon it the obligation to make the Gospel known. This state of affairs is constant wherever two or three are gathered together in the name of Christ; it does not temporarily lapse if a parish is without a priest.

191.   When Anglican congregations develop this idea in the direction of having elders and local priests it is not surprising that fears are voiced of an incipient congregationalism. The Church of England is by conviction an episcopal Church. That does not simply mean that we possess a senior rank among the clergy called bishops; it expresses an understanding of oversight *(episcope)* which, by being vested in the Bishop and shared with his priests, relates local groups to each other and to the whole Church. The Bishop is thus an essential focus of the Church's unity and catholicity. At the same time participation in the ecumenical movement should by now have taught us that congregationalism contains an important element of the truth about the local Church. If it is to be faithful to its calling it must seek out and recognise its own ministry. This will include the task of oversight and leadership *within* the local Church.

WHO ARE THE LEADERS?
192.   Charge of a parish is committed by the Bishop to an incumbent. He is generally a stranger in the parish when he arrives, and the average duration of his tenure is currently about six years. He may, in a few parishes, enjoy the assistance of a junior priest who remains for an even shorter period of time. In some places there are now non-stipendiary priests who help with parochial duties and are a fixture unless required to move for reasons of secular employment. This is seen as a problem because the NSM may not relate well to a new leader when there is a change of incumbent. It is felt that the position of authority given to the latter must be safeguarded. Under the Synodical Government Measure the incumbent and the parochial church council share a duty 'to consult together on matters of general concern and importance to the parish'. It is the function of the PCC to co-operate with the

115

incumbent 'in promoting in the parish the whole mission of the church, pastoral, evangelistic, social and ecumenical'. Churchwardens are officers of the Bishop. In a certain sense, therefore, they share a delegated oversight; they are 'foremost in representing the laity and in co-operating with the incumbent'.[1] The existing picture of leadership in the local Church, as just described, allows for shared ministry and indeed requires a degree of co-operation. But in practice both priest and people, more often than not, operate the system as one which is designed to make consultation and assistance available to the *one* leader, the incumbent. It is thus regarded as a clerical support system–

'For P.C.C.'s were really made
To give your local vicar aid.'

(John Betjeman)

THE NEED FOR CHANGE

193.   Channelling authority and leadership through one man in the local Church has been severely criticised on a number of grounds. It places a limit on church growth, since there is a maximum number of people to whom one person can relate in the sort of depth necessary for effective pastoral ministry. It puts unreasonable expectations on the leader, since no one person possesses all the gifts which are required for building up the Church. It creates the impression that lay ministry is purely supplementary and secondary to ordained ministry. David Watson has likened the vicar in this approach to a bottleneck:

'Nothing can go in or out except through him. No meetings can take place unless he is the leader or chairman. No decisions can be made without his counsel or approach. This bottle concept of the church makes growth and maturity virtually impossible. Members are unable to develop into the God-given ministry they could well experience because, in structure and in practice, there is room for only one minister.'[2]

194.   It is undeniable that the system has in the past allowed some very remarkable priests to flourish. Moreover it can be very comforting to individual parishioners in a small enough parish to feel that they are known and cared for by a particular pastor. But the shape of the ministry must reflect the needs of the Church; and it is a serious weakness to have to perpetuate the one-man parish with present numbers of full-time priests. They become desperately overstretched. The local Church must be challenged to undertake ministry. Individuals will be much more adequately cared for through shared ministry, and the intimate relationship of the small parish can be reproduced in providing lay pastors for house groups or specific areas.

195.   Three factors in particular have drawn attention to the possibilities of shared leadership in recent years. These are: the need to build a truly

indigenous Church in urban priority areas; the disappearance of the resident parson from many villages; and the need to provide adequate pastoral care where there is a large population and a growing Church. Between them these three factors are relevant to the majority of parishes in the Church of England today. But in addition to these, the influence of the charismatic movement has made the whole Church much more aware of the contribution which every member makes to ministry. Among the laity it is quite clear that the Holy Spirit has provided gifts of pastoring and leadership which are simply lost if the clergy 'bottleneck' persists, or they may find an outlet in separatist fellowships and house churches.

PATTERNS OF LEADERSHIP

196. If our concern is with the local Church then it seems clear that different patterns of leadership will be appropriate in different places, because the size of the Church, the nature of the community in which it is set, the varying availability of gifts within the congregation, and the emphases of its mission will all vary. Where the Church is weak it will continue to depend largely upon imported ministry using resources which are available in deanery and diocese. A team of deacons and priests might be committed over a number of years to a whole area which is lacking in indigenous ministry. No strategy could sensibly propose the disappearance of the 'sole cure' overnight. But it *is* the ultimate strategy of these proposals, not to provide an incumbent for every parish, but to see every stipendiary priest as a provider of external resources and vision for the local Church's own ministry. One, or more than one, such priest in every parish would be of immense advantage; it is vital that every parish continues to have access to such resources, and for more maintained priests of this sort to be available.

197. But this re-interpretation of the full-time priest's role does mean turning on its head what is often supposed to be one of the principal reasons for appointing leaders in the local Church, whatever title they are given. They are seen as a support group for the clergy, to deliver them from isolation and barrenness in their ministry. Instead, the full-time priest should be seen as a support for the local Church with its indigenous ministry. Naturally he will also need support himself, as is indicated here by a preference for the term 'maintained' rather than 'stipendiary', because it includes reference to more than financial provision. Much of this personal support will of course come from the local Church leaders because there is always a partnership in ministry. But in terms of the task, the mission of the Church, that is the local Church's responsibility and the maintained priest who gets involved in it is not there to direct, but to provide resources and support; asking questions and challenging assumptions as necessary, but always in order to make the local leadership more aware of its responsibilities. There are three available patterns of local leadership which will be considered here: the parochial church council, a local eldership, and a local priesthood.

198.   The PCC is the properly constituted body for bearing day to day responsibility in the local Church. It is accountable to the annual church meeting. Answers to questions from the diocese about the life of the parish and the policy of the local Church, especially from the archdeacon as the Bishop's officer in these matters, are expected to reflect discussion in the PCC; it is a failure in consultation if the incumbent and churchwardens reply without reference to the Council. As has been noted above, the terms of reference of the PCC are most certainly not limited to administration and finance. It should be the body which determines the Church's missionary policy, its forms of worship, and the Christian nurture of its members.

199.   It was argued in a previous chapter that a principal step towards implementing this or any other strategy for ministry should be the requirement that each PCC assesses the ministerial resources and needs of its own parish with consultancy help from the diocese. The report on *The Charismatic Movement in the Church in England* was therefore right to see a danger in the setting up in some Churches of a leadership group separate from the PCC:

> 'An over-simplistic interpretation of the New Testament emphases on the local, permanent and supervisory nature of "eldership" has led to a widespread notion of "lay elders". In places this has issued in a desire to *add* this element to Anglican structures of, e.g. vicar, curate, lay reader, wardens and PCC. It is often easier to add such an office than it is to define its powers and responsibilities over against existing offices.'[3]

200.   Nothing should be proposed in the Church of England which would take away or by-pass the duties of the PCC, not just because it is there, but because it needs to be there, as an elected and representative body accountable to the whole membership. As it normally functions, however, it is not ideally suited to all leadership tasks. The formation of policy is clearly part of its brief: detailed pastoral oversight is another matter. The PCC needs to include representation of all areas of Church life through membership of the council or its committees. It is therefore too large and diffuse a body, and meets too infrequently, to cope with the ever-changing and highly personalised demands of pastoral care. Responsibility in this area could be given to a group which functions in effect as a committee of the PCC: or another model is available.

A LOCAL ELDERSHIP

201.   The Church of England is quite accustomed to the existence of staff groups alongside representative bodies. A deanery chapter meeting is not the house of clergy of the deanery synod in session. A team ministry necessitates close co-operation and planning between a staff group in addition to parochial and district council meetings. Incumbents of large parishes

regularly gather together any curates, deaconesses, lay workers, and often readers as well, for discussions about their shared ministry. At diocesan level the Bishop needs a staff meeting as well as his council and his synod. There is therefore no reason why a local Church which accepts its responsibilities for its own ministry should not have a group which works together as a ministerial leadership team and reports to the PCC as the body responsible for policy decisions.

202.   Such a group is preferable to an individual because it allows the contribution of different gifts and styles of leadership, and it also makes possible a sharing of pastoral care when large numbers of people are involved. It is not irrelevant to notice that leadership of the local Church in the New Testament always appears as something shared by a group, and there was an obvious precedent for that in the board of elders of the synagogue (cf. Acts 13.15; 14.23).

203.   Should a similar group today be called 'the elders'? A survey of 23 parishes with local leadership schemes revealed ten variations on the title used.[4] Two dioceses have adopted schemes for appointing 'elders'. A problem with this word is the etymological link with the presbyterate. 'Lay elders' on this basis are a contradiction in terms, and ordination is not generally envisaged. The United Reformed Church has elders whose office is described in similar terms to the sort of local leadership we are thinking of, but they are given a form of ordination:

> 'They share with ministers of the Word and Sacraments in the pastoral oversight and leadership of the local churches, taking counsel together in the Elders' Meeting for the whole Church and having each a group of members particularly entrusted to his pastoral care. They shall be associated with ministers in all the Councils of the Church. Elders, elected by the Church Meeting, are ordained to their office and are inducted to serve for such limited period as the Church which elects them shall determine.'[5]

One way through the difficulties of terminology in the Church of England might be to refer to the leadership group in the local Church corporately as 'the eldership', but that it should be composed individually of priests, deacons and lay pastors. However, deciding what such a group should be called is less important than determining its functions, its methods of working, and its relationship to the PCC, to the whole local community, and to the Bishop.

MINISTRY OF WORD AND SACRAMENTS

204.   The primary responsibility of the eldership should be to ensure that an appropriate ministry of Word and Sacrament is provided in the parish. They will not necessarily fulfil this ministry themselves. They will seek to identify and encourage the gifts of others within the Church, and they will make use as necessary of other ministerial resources within the deanery and

the diocese. They will be prepared to undergo training themselves, and attend to the training needs of all those who are entered on the Church's 'ministry roll'. Where the local Church includes house groups, the leaders of these and ministry in them will either be provided or supervised by the eldership. Special attention needs to be given to the quality of the Church's teaching ministry, and the eldership should be particularly accountable to the Bishop for their development of this at all levels and for all ages of Church membership. If house groups share in the Eucharist they should only do so with an elder presiding, just as the local Church always breaks the one bread in fellowship with the Bishop or his delegated presbyter.

LAY PRESIDENCY AT THE EUCHARIST

205. This raises the question of whether, if lay pastors are to be associated with priests and deacons in local Church eldership, it should not be possible for them to preside at the Eucharist? The shortage of sacramental ministers in rural areas, and the desire of many house groups to share in eucharistic worship, have created a call for more 'eucharistizers' to be available. It is pointed out that nothing in the New Testament limits presiding at the Lord's table to one particular kind of minister, and that the full training provided for the priesthood is hardly necessary to equip someone to carry out this duty in a worthy manner. It is perhaps something which should naturally be associated with leadership in the local Church. A letter to the *Church Times* expressed this point of view clearly:

> 'What the present situation requires...is that it should be possible for an authorised lay minister...who holds a position of leadership within a local church to be empowered to act as deputy- or vice-president when the normal president is not available–e.g. during illness, absence or an interregnum.'[6]

206. However, the difficulty with which we are faced in the Church today is one where the number of 'normal presidents' available is not just temporarily insufficient, but likely to remain so. We are not making emergency arrangements, but planning a strategy for adequate future ministry. Even if the Bishop might authorise lay presidency where temporary difficulties made it necessary for the Church's welfare; even if, in extreme situations the local Church, lacking contact with its Bishop, could appoint one of its own number to this ministry, it does not follow that there exists a theological case for making lay presidency part of this strategy. For that purpose, it would be necessary to establish that lay leaders in the local Church should in *principle* have authority to preside at the Eucharist. But how would one distinguish theologically between the recognition of that authority and ordination? We are arguing in this report that the harmful clergy-laity divide in the Church will not be overcome by abolishing distinctions between the two, but by regarding the clergy as members of the laity, who are authorised to represent the whole laity, both in their public ministry, and in their representative functions within the Christian community. Presidency at the Eucharist is

120

undeniably a representative function: it should accordingly be entrusted to those who represent the priestly ministry of the whole Body. Instead of lay pastors therefore, should the local eldership consist of a local priesthood?

A LOCAL PRIESTHOOD

207.   We have already paid some attention to the widespread discussion in the Church at the moment about the idea of a local priesthood. We have examined the reasons for this interest, and some of the hazards of introducing a two-level presbyterate. We have described what might appropriately be some of the distinctive functions of diocesan and of local priests. At this point a fresh perspective on the debate may be suggested. Attention is concentrated on the need to find local priests in places where maintained priests or lay leaders are in short supply, such as the deep countryside or urban priority areas. Even if successful, the tendency will inevitably be towards the creation of a second-class priesthood for second-class parishes. The emphasis of this report upon the need for *every* local Church to under-take responsibility for its ministry includes in principle the calling out of a local priesthood. It follows that a form of ministry which might appear in any parish (just as readers at present might be found in any parish) would not become the sort of inverted status symbol which is feared in view of the differences of training and function which would be bound to exist between the two kinds of priest. The local priest would find his proper context in the local Church's provision of its own leadership; the diocesan priest would find his proper context as part of the Bishop's provision of ministry in the diocese.

208.   But should the entire eldership of a local Church be ordained to the priesthood? A number of reasons suggest that this is not desirable:

i) It would increase expectations upon the eldership and therefore make it more difficult to establish at the outset.

ii) It would exclude some (including e.g. some readers) with gifts to be lay pastors, but no life-long vocation to the priesthood.

iii) Because fewer would feel called it would make it more difficult to establish a corporate leadership in smaller Churches.

iv) A mixed eldership would make it clear that a local priest operates as part of a team.

v) Local priests would be best trained as part of a mixed ministerial team.

vi) Deacons would relate less well to an eldership composed entirely of priests.

209.   Although the eldership would possess a representative function and be responsible for the welfare of the whole Church (both of which indicate presbyteral ministry), this would not have to be true of each individual

member of the eldership. Obviously each member would share to some degree in oversight, but the concept of oversight is one which includes a scale of gradation, and it would be ridiculous to suggest that anyone with any kind of pastoral responsibility in the Church should be in orders. The shared leadership of the local Church could readily include lay pastors who were not presidents of the Eucharist, as it could also include priests who did not act as chairmen of committees:

> 'The essence of shared ministry is that it allows the gifts that people have to develop without guilt and frustration about the abilities they lack.'[7]

THE APPOINTMENT OF THE ELDERSHIP

210.   In the appointment of the eldership in the local Church the two governing principles which we have followed in this strategy must be brought together. If the PCC is ready to review its needs and resources in ministry with consultancy help provided by the diocese it will among other things consider the gifts of leadership which are available. Local ministry is called out by the local Church. At the same time the Bishop's responsibility to care for the flock needs to be expressed in some relationship equivalent to the 'my cure and yours' which is found in the institution of an incumbent, or understood in the installation of a priest-in-charge. One or more presbyters, acting in association with the Bishop in the local Church, are therefore necessary to preside at the Eucharist and to work with the leaders of the local Church in the eldership. That does not mean, however, that presbyters must have a monopoly of leadership functions. It does mean that if there is no local presbyter, no-one in the local Church whom the Bishop can associate with his own ministry, then the Bishop must provide someone from among his diocesan priests. In this way local and episcopal responsibilities would always be held together.

211.   The Bishop of Winchester, in a talk on local ministry given to the Southern Regional Institute, suggested that 'the principle ought to be established that responsibility for each unit of the church lies in the hands of that unit'. At the same time, 'the local unit is saved from sectarianism by episcopacy'. Pressure ought to be resisted for a quick decision about individual candidates for a local priesthood. In his stimulating discussion of the future of rural ministry, Christopher Newton envisaged one model in which an eldership team existed for at least five years before an ordination was possible.[8] A consultation in January 1982 organised by the diocese of Lichfield for dioceses considering a local ordained ministry suggested several stages in the appointment process:

  i) An initial consultation between the Bishop, or his representative, and the local Church. Some pastoral units might not be ready for development towards local ministry.

  ii) A local election (by the PCC or church meeting) of a mixed leadership group. The parish priest 'discerns the result'.

iii) Training of a mixed group.

iv) Possible emergence of candidates for a local priesthood, who would then need to have their vocation assessed by the wider Church.[9]

Further attention will be given to questions of selection and training in later chapters.

212.  It is no part of the idea of a local priesthood that it should be in some way outside catholic order, any more than the local Church is distinct from the Church catholic. Both are a particular manifestation of the catholic Church and priesthood. The differences between local and diocesan priests should be seen in terms of appointment, training and function, not in ordination or association with the Bishop. In view of the particular discernment of gifts leading to the ordination of local priests it is unlikely that many of them would be called to become diocesan priests, although it is certainly possible that some would be made aware of a wider vocation by this route. Before undertaking the work of a diocesan priest a local priest would clearly need to undergo further processes of selection and training, but no further ordination. This would in no sense imply that the local priesthood is in some way 'inferior'; further selection and training either is or should be the invariable rule when a priest transfers from one type of work to another.

THE HAZARDS OF LOCAL LEADERSHIP

213.  A pattern of ministry which puts so much emphasis upon the initiative and responsibility of the local Church is bound to meet certain obvious objections among which there are perhaps four of particular force.

*(1) Its Permanence*

There is no reason why lay members of the eldership should not serve for a limited term. Those in orders will of course remain a permanent part of the leadership in their Church until they either resign or move. There are hazards in this admittedly, just as it is extremely hazardous to give an incumbent the freehold tenure of his benefice—an example of potential permanence with few parallels! It is true that incumbents must now retire, but it could also be the practice for local priests to have temporary licences. Generally speaking it could be argued that the local Church is liable to suffer more from the comings and goings of incumbents than it would from a continuous leadership team which never resigns *en bloc*.

*(2) Its Parochialism*

This would be no new problem for the local Church. Every eldership, however many local priests were available, should continue to include ministers from outside, whether diocesan priests or deacons. They might be heavily involved in the pastoral work of that Church; they might have a specialist ministry in the area; or they might simply attend eldership meetings as diocesan consultants. In every case their role would include bringing into the local Church leadership the vision of the wider Church and of mission to the community.

### (3) Its Potential for Party Spirit

All communities contain the seeds of division. The New Testament provides sufficient evidence that the Church is not exempt. There is a usefulness in the introduction from outside the community of an independent, reconciling figure. The parochial clergy at present frequently find themselves in this position, especially in rural parishes because 'members of small communities find it harder to avoid conflicts within the tightly woven web of social relationships'.[10] But is the existence of polarised groups requiring the presence of the vicar as a referee a true image of the Gospel society? Through a leadership team the local community would be challenged to work together, and the contribution of an independent outsider would still be available from among the diocesan priests and deacons.

### (4) Its Lack of Professionalism

We have already considered what is meant by 'professionalism' in ministry. There is a professionalism appropriate to each particular kind of ministry; there is a professionalism appropriate to ordained ministry; there is a professionalism appropriate to maintained ministry of any kind; and there is a professionalism appropriate to all who 'profess and call themselves Christians'. The points at issue here are whether those called to leadership in the local Church would be prepared to equip themselves to fulfil their ministry, and whether those looking to them for leadership would understand what they might properly expect from them.

EXPECTATIONS UPON LOCAL MINISTRY

214.   Initially the expectations placed upon the local leadership, and local priests in particular, are likely to cause problems. There may well be an assumption where there is only one local priest available that he is supposed to do his best to undertake the duties of an incumbent. Even if it is appreciated by Church members that his responsibilities are now shared by the eldership as a whole, there may be many in the community who continue to expect the priest to be their 'access point' to the world of faith and the city of God. For this purpose an individual is much more identifiable than a group.

215.   The resulting portmanteau of expectations likely to be borne by a local priest may be divided into what people think he should do; what people think he should know; and what people think he should be. What he does should be the subject of corporate decision within the local Church, in the light of agreed policies about who should be involved, for example, in

124

baptism or marriage preparation, or in bereavement counselling. As for a local priest's knowledge, that should clearly include a number of things essential to all presbyteral ministry; but there are various kinds of knowledge. A local priest may not have as much knowledge of historical theology as a colleague who has read for a degree, but he will probably know more about how people live in his own area. The local Church needs to use a variety of resources and it will be liberating for the priest not to be regarded as the source of all wisdom.

216.   The most difficult area is what people expect the priest to be. A survey of attitudes in one diocese emphasised trust, confidentiality and professionalism as things lay people valued in a vicar. This may make it difficult for them to accept the priestly ministry of somebody who is already a familiar member of the community. However, the ministry of many non-stipendiaries bears witness to the fact that it is possible for the home-grown priest to win acceptance among friends and neighbours, and even to enjoy certain advantages in communication over the full-time priest in the vicarage. At the same time it will be helpful for a local priest to have available diocesan priests who provide pastoral counselling and spiritual direction when an unknown face is needed. Insofar as it is the role of the priest to help people to cope with their need for dependence it may be claimed that such teamwork between local and diocesan priests could provide greater versatility than is normally at present available in the average parish. At the end of the day, however, it will only be possible to meet the demands of ministry where a local Church is able to grow under the care of a corporate leadership in which the diversity of the Spirit's gifts are fully recognised.

NOTES TO CHAPTER 15: LEADERSHIP IN THE LOCAL CHURCH

[1]Canon E1.4.
[2]D. Watson, *I Believe in the Church*, Hodder and Stoughton, 1978, p.246.
[3]*The Charismatic Movement in the Church of England*, CIO Publishing, 1981, p.37.
[4]C. Bevington, *Shared Leadership in the Local Church*, A project prepared for a course at St George's House, Windsor, January 1983, p.28.
[5]*Basis of Union of the United Reformed Church*, 1972.
[6]*Church Times*, 21st January 1983.
[7]C. Bevington, *op.cit.*, p.34.
[8]C. Newton, *Life and Death in the Country Church*, p.6f.
[9]See *Report of a Consultation Concerning the Local Ordained Ministry*, Lichfield Diocese/ Shallowford, January 1982, p.12.
[10]P. Wignall, *Taking Custody of the Future*, Oxford Institute for Church and Society, 1982, p.4.

# 16: Resources for the Local Church

217.    The picture which has been drawn in the previous chapter of a leadership team in each local Church, with a structure of lay pastors caring for related house groups and local priests called out from their number to serve the Church in teaching and sacramental ministry, may seem quite unrealistic for the majority of parishes. It may be assumed that it could be applied only to eclectic city-centre congregations, and to parishes in some of the more prosperous parts of suburbia and the medium-sized towns. In most places the Church is simply too weak, it might be argued, and lacking in resources to provide its own ministry in this way.

218.    In the midst of the deep sense of defeatism which has descended on some Anglican parishes, causing the faithful to settle for survival rather than growth, we need to hear a voice from outside, from those with far fewer privileges and advantages than we take for granted. Among many that might be listened to I recall one from Mozambique. In 1979 the Anglican cathedral there and all the main churches were closed following the Marxist revolution; schools and hospitals were taken over; teaching or baptising children, open-air and house services were forbidden; contact with the outside world was almost severed. How does the Church do its work when deprived of so many of its traditional resources? Bishop Dinis Sengulane has described the response in this case:

> 'In 1980 we had a synod. (Sic!) After much prayer on evangelism we took a decision which would involve everybody. Each member should feel that the minimum he could do was to bring one person to Christ every year.
>
> 'Then we thought of having something visible to help start off conversations, so we went back to the fish symbol . . . Of course you know that ICHTHUS–FISH in Greek–has the initial letters of JESUS CHRIST, SON OF GOD, SAVIOUR. So we are trying to get every member of our Church to wear this fish wherever they go. If anybody asks them what it is, they say: "Well, Jesus Christ is my Saviour. I wonder what your position is about him?" '[1]

In addition to personal testimony there has been a lay initiative for a monthly day of prayer and fasting, when a collection of food and clothing is made for the starving poor. During these years there has been a remarkable growth in the Church: in one place where the building was closed in 1979 and the congregation had been about 80 strong, the Bishop recently confirmed 500 people; this was his third confirmation there in twelve months.

219.    By comparison the average English parish is rich in terms of buildings, money, education and freedom from oppression. For us the primary need is

not to meet deficiencies in manpower or training for ministry, but to seek the spiritual resources of faith and hope and love which have been so evident in the Church in Mozambique during the time of its trial. Without these of course it will be hopeless to expect a strategy to be effective which is based upon the acceptance by the local Church of its responsibilities for mission. This was well expressed by Herbert Kelly, founder of the Society for the Sacred Mission, who was advocating local ministry sixty years ago, when he said 'You can't expect an A1 ministry from a C3 church.'[2]

DISCOVERING THE LOCAL CHURCH'S MISSION

220.    Another form of defeatism can be induced by comparing the Church's resources with the size of its mission. Reports are merely depressing if they catalogue the myriad ways in which individuals and congregations could usefully concern themselves with the life of the community in the name of Christ. There is no end to what might be done in theory; the question is to know what God actually wants this group of believers to be doing now. An interesting American workbook on the ministry of the laity has made this point under a heading 'Strategy for Ministry':

> 'Our ministry is frequently overwhelmed by too many needs and pressures or by not seeing exactly where and how to begin. Without focus, a place to begin, or a place on which to build, our energies are diffused and are finally lost ... Specific goals which are realistic, tangible, and yet challenging should take into account our individual strengths and limitations. Most of all, such strategy for ministry does not leave out the element of faith, of God's presence not only in our successes but also in our failures.'[3]

221.    The strategy with which we are concerned must therefore go further than loading the local Church with the weight of responsibility for mission. It must suggest a place to begin, or rather on which to build since the mission in many parishes is well over a thousand years old. In seeking such a place it is helpful to ask what does already exist by way of resources, what are the occupations, the skills and the concerns of those who are ready to be included on the 'ministry roll'? These will provide obvious openings for mission. Sometimes there may be locally an issue or a situation where it is imperative for the testimony to Jesus Christ to be given, but no-one in the congregation may feel qualified or in a position to make it. This is where co-operation through deanery mission committees and the assistance of diocesan ministry teams are important to this strategy. But the Christian mission can be picked up anywhere by people using what they already have. Indeed it is fundamental to this mission, which became apparent through a process of incarnation, that God actually prepares the context, as well as calls the Church to operate within those limits; so that context, those limits, are not just difficulties: they spell out the opportunities for us which God himself is providing. If these are being fully grasped there is no need to worry about the hypothetical list of activities which could be attempted under the heading of mission.

222.   Our working definition of ministry distinguishes between ministry *in* the Church and the ministry *of* the Church. The purpose of the former is summed up in St Paul's description of the need for the Church to be 'built up in love' (Ephesians 4.16). What it requires in order to do this is to receive the apostolic teaching, to share the common life *(koinonia)*, to break bread and to pray (Acts 2.42). Ministry in the Church will therefore be concerned to provide for all of these activities. It is a ministry of word and sacraments, of prayer and pastoral care. Shared ministry includes the participation of every church member in this, not merely as recipient but also as contributor. Each will certainly contribute best by making use of his or her particular gifts. One ministry there is, however, which is laid upon all by clear injunction over and over again in the New Testament: it is prayer.

## THE MINISTRY OF PRAYER

223.   Intercession is the major priestly work of the people of God. Within the liturgy the prayers arise from the congregation, and one or more of the laity may express their common requests. There are some who know themselves called especially to a ministry of prayer. It can be the thankful task of housebound saints. The religious communities sustain this service of God. Generally speaking, an awareness of a call to prayer is one of the most significant features of the developing ministry of the laity. Every local Church, every PCC, every house group or cell, needs to give the attention to this ministry which it so evidently had in the mission of Jesus. In a multitude of ways the Church is discovering afresh that all things work by prayer. Perhaps there is a call here to the religious communities to be more fully available to local Churches, not only to provide places and leaders for retreats, but also to send out teachers in the school of prayer, and to make their own prayer-centred communities a resource for others.

224.   Prayer includes the praise of God. For this, the specialist ministry of those who have musical gifts is of great significance. Their help is needed in raising what is still generally a feeble standard of congregational praise through song. Attention is often concentrated on the emotive area of musical style rather than on the wider subject of enabling the whole congregation to worship. But praise is not something to be confined to the sanctuary. It is one thing for Christians to be inspired by singing rousing hymns: it is another for this rejoicing in God to be evident in the life of each believer. The Church, as a royal priesthood, is to proclaim the praises of God to the whole world (1 Peter 2.9).

## PASTORS AND TEACHERS

225.   Among the gifts of ministry for the Church mentioned in Ephesians pastors and teachers are linked together. It may be implied that every pastor

is a teacher and vice versa. Of course there are, and will continue to be, people with specialist gifts in education; just as there are pastors whose ministry of the Word does not include formal teaching and preaching. But the regular ministry of teaching in a local Church is inseparable from its pastoral needs. This is so clear that it is amazing how seldom there is any consultation about a teaching plan or subjects for sermons, and how there is equally little attempt to organise any group discussion of or response to preaching. As Mark Gibbs puts it:

> 'Christian proclamation is more than a matter of enunciating unquestionable dogmas; the art of Christian learning, like the art of worship, is surely something a parish must take great trouble over.'[4]

Teaching is really an aspect of pastoral ministry. Like other aspects it is something to be shared in the local Church, but it is right that local priests, who are ordained to a ministry of Word and Sacraments, should be able to play a part in this work and not be regarded as dispensers of the Sacraments alone. It is a historic part of the understanding of ministry in the reformed Church of England that there is an essential wholeness about the ministry of Word and Sacraments. Furthermore, the kind of person of maturity in Christ who is envisaged as suitable for the local priesthood must in the nature of the case be someone whose life has been formed by the Word of God.

THE MINISTRY OF READERS

226.    It is in relation to the ministry of pastoring and teaching that the existing office of Reader in the Church of England must be considered. Numerically, readers are of very great significance as they are far and away the largest category of accredited ministry in the Church apart from the stipendiary priesthood. At the beginning of 1982 there were 6,759 on the active list, or roughly two for every three full-time priests in parochial ministry. In 1981 the number of readers admitted to ministry (421) well exceeded the number of those ordained to the stipendiary ministry (311), and was not far short of the total ordained, including NSMs (440). Readers cost the Church very little, yet most enquiries reveal that many of them consider that they are under-used.[5] Partly this has been the result of changes in the forms of worship in many parishes: fewer non-sacramental services means that the presence of a priest is usually necessary, while many other lay people now undertake liturgical duties formerly reserved to the clergy and readers. Nevertheless, this feeling of under-employment may be linked to two major problems about readers' ministry.

227.    The first is that the Church has in the past invested far too little money and care in the training of readers. Their own sense of morale is high enough in many cases to prompt readers to a diligent stewardship in their ministry, and standards are now generally being improved, but recent reports indicate that there is still some way to go.[6] If some readers are under-employed it

may be because the Church has licensed to its preaching and teaching ministry some who are insufficiently equipped to fulfil it.

228.   The second problem lies in the uncertainty which exists over how readers should best be used. One diocese has noted how they are seen as a kind of second-best substitute for occasions when a priest is not available:

> 'In these circumstances many Readers are being used as peripatetic preachers and are seldom in their own parish churches. Thus they seldom hear anyone else preach; they lack the spiritual support of membership of a team, and the spiritual development of a regular pattern of worship of their own. They have no opportunity of fitting into a proper place in the teaching role of the Church, and it is largely for these reasons that the image of the Reader is not that of a vital and effective member of the ministerial team within the local worshipping community.'[7]

In their own report on strategy the Readers' Committee have recognised that the development of a shared local ministry has sometimes left readers on one side in their traditional 'stopgap' role. They see the need 'to ask not how the Reader will fit into this developing and/or future pattern, but what pattern of ministry the Church needs to develop and is there a place for the Reader within it?'[8]

229.   Whether it is measured in terms of numbers or of commitment the potential contribution of the ministry of readers to a future strategy is very great indeed. Their existence encourages a hope that the local ministry is something which could be established quite quickly in many parishes, and for this reason the strategy here proposed accords with the report of the Readers' Committee in suggesting that 'the Reader of the future . . . would be a Local Minister'.[9] Those men and women who at present are encouraged to train for reader ministry (and there were 1,714 in training in 1982, compared to 1,129 training for ordination) would in most cases be among those who could fulfil their ministry in a local eldership or leadership team. Some might be candidates for the local priesthood; others would be included as lay pastors in the eldership. It has been pointed out that where there is a suitable reader already trained to preach the Word and proven to be an acceptable pastor there is a strong case for calling such a person to a local sacramental ministry as well. Whether the title of reader should be continued for those who retain their lay vocation (and the Committee's report considers that 'the name is clearly inappropriate') is a question which could be left to each local Church, because readers would not continue to be a separate quasi-order nationally but would be merged into the local ministry. In some places a separate name to indicate those lay pastors who have been trained for a preaching and teaching ministry might be thought desirable, but if so the title of 'lay preacher' would be more descriptive. Some readers might see their ministry as something much wider than leadership in one particular local Church. If this calling has substance they ought to be selected and

trained for the Order of Deacon, and serve as something akin to public preachers.

230.   There are other ways in which local ministry is clearly developing at present. The regular pastoral work of the parish priest has in many places of necessity become largely restricted to those who are at home during the day, to the sick and the bereaved, and to those who call at the parsonage door. Even regular worshippers who are out at work on weekdays may seldom receive a visit from the clergy because of other pressures. The scheme for a lay pastorate at Christ Church, Purley, for example, sprang from a realisation that those for whom pastoral care ought to be most readily available are often those seen least regularly in church, and about whose needs one is least likely to hear. There are, therefore, numerous cries for help which are never heard. Within the body of Christ there is a ministry of listening for these cries, as well as one of practical skill in bringing help, and a gift of speaking the word of healing or of encouragement. And these ministries are inter-dependent, for

'Thou didst ears and hands and voices
For thy praise design.'

Street wardens, visiting teams, house group leaders, organisers of practical help–whatever forms the lay pastorate may take should be left to each local Church to decide. Local ministries are local precisely because they reflect the varying needs of each locality.

ACCREDITATION

231.   The Accredited Lay Ministry Committee of ACCM carried out at the end of 1981 an enquiry into the extent of episcopally authorised ministry in each diocese. This revealed that in various places accreditation is given to a wide range of ministries beyond those authorised by the Bishop's licence (viz. readers, deaconesses, licensed lay workers and Church Army officers). These include church social workers, pastoral auxiliaries, stewardship advisers, and lay people authorised to administer communion. It is clear that there is no common policy regarding the appropriate form of authorisation and which ministries require diocesan accreditation. Some dioceses are opposed to the multiplication of different offices. The line adopted in this strategy is that where a lay ministry serves the whole diocese (e.g. steward-ship adviser) it should be considered for inclusion in the diaconate; all local lay ministries should be recognised locally and require no further authorisation.

NOTES TO CHAPTER 16: RESOURCES FOR THE LOCAL CHURCH

[1] *Friends of USPG Newsletter*, Summer 1982, p.3.

[2] Quoted in V. Strudwick, 'Local Ordained Ministry: Yesterday's Case for Tomorrow's Church', *Theology*, May 1981, pp.170–76.

[3] N. Vox, *Monday's Ministries: The Ministry of the Laity*, ed. R. Tiemeyer, Parish Life Press, Philadelphia, 1979, p.60.

[4] M. Gibbs, *Christians with Secular Power*, Laity Exchange Books, Fortress Press, Philadelphia, 1981, p.39.

[5] See e.g. *Report of the Working Party on the Changing Patterns of the Ministry of Readers*, Ripon Diocesan Readers' Board, 1976.

[6] See e.g. *Shared Ministry, The Report of the Working Party on Ministry made to the Bishop of St Edmundsbury and Ipswich*, Dec. 1980, p.19; and *Strategy for Ministry: Report of a Readers' Committee Working Group*, 1982, p.8. The latter report, which was produced by the Readers' Committee partly to assist me in the preparation of my material, and to which I am indebted, makes the following observation: 'The provisions of the General Readers' Certificate clearly require each and every diocese to make provisions for an adequate and appropriate training scheme for candidates in training. The response has been far from uniform . . . Most diocesan schemes are very conservative in their approach . . . Most have not accepted the insights of the (GRC) syllabus.'

[7] Diocese of Southwell Ministry Commission, *A Working Paper on the Use of Readers*, June 1981, p.6f.

[8] *Op.cit.*, p.18.

[9] *Ibid.*, p.22.

# IMPLICATIONS

# 17: Ways of Structuring Ministry

232.   The strategy which has now been outlined has numerous implications for ministerial structures, selection and training. However these will be described rather tentatively and without much detail. It is the function of a strategy to suggest a general line of development without entering into all possible ramifications. Important though it is to anticipate any fatal obstacles which may await an attempt to implement the strategy, it is also necessary to allow a degree of flexibility so that there is freedom to respond to unforeseen changes. This is especially the case when a period as long as forty years is required for the strategy to take full effect.

PATRONAGE AND THE PARSON'S FREEHOLD

233.   One major reason why the time-scale is of this length may be found in the existing legal rights of those who possess either an advowson or a benefice. This strategy, like that of Leslie Paul twenty years ago, requires the abolition of patronage. There is no room for a third party if the local Church is to call out its own ministry and the Bishop as chief pastor is looked to as the person responsible for providing outside resources. The clergy freehold would be replaced by a system of having priests and deacons on a diocesan establishment similar to that envisaged in the Fenton Morley Report as described in Chapter 2. A great deal of work has been done over the past twenty years with regard to the legal arrangements concerning appointments to benefices, even though no major reform has so far proved to be acceptable. Apart from the difficulty of achieving a consensus in the Church, there is also the complication that the rights of the Crown are closely involved. Nothing less than complete abolition, not merely of private patronage, but of the patronage system will ultimately satisfy the requirements of this strategy, although of course a piecemeal approach is possible. That point is particularly important in addressing the formidable task of removing the freehold. Even supposing this to be achieved, there is no possibility that the rights of existing incumbents would be taken away. That alone means a period of at least twenty years during which the number of benefices would gradually diminish. These implications are merely noted here. Whether they constitute a fatal deterrent to the strategy will be considered in the final section.

TEAM AND GROUP MINISTRIES

234.   One modification of the benefice system has come about through the development of teams and groups under the Pastoral Measure of 1968. They

135

are the subject of a current working party which may in due course recommend some changes in the methods of establishment and operation of these forms of collaborative ministry. It is a difficult task to assess the effectiveness of teams and groups. It is well known that team ministries have a tendency to run into difficulties, although it is seldom asked whether other styles of ministry simply avoid difficulties which should be faced, especially in the area of collaboration in mission. Apart from personality clashes the chief problems of teams appear to centre around the continuing significance of the benefice. The diocesan ministry teams proposed in this strategy would avoid all contact with anything resembling a benefice. The priests and deacons composing them would have contracts of employment relating to the job descriptions drawn up at the time of their appointment. As a consequence the stipendiary clergy of the Church of England would become unambiguously employed persons. This may be regarded as the final threat to their professional status, and it would undoubtedly entail some loss of privilege. But their traditional position as office holders has become increasingly difficult to sustain in the face of modern legislation and this is a matter in which it is impossible ultimately to have one's cake and eat it. Moreover, the diocesan ministry teams would be defined in terms of their specialist tasks and the questions of roles and relationships would be clarified in the light of this.

235. Group ministries do not encounter the same difficulties, but there are far fewer groups than teams under the Pastoral Measure, and no great number of new ones is under active consideration at present. There is of course no reason why parishes should not operate informally in a group relationship, and it would be possible to propose removing group ministries entirely from the Measure. In fact the early group ministries in Norwich diocese preceded the legislation. Their arrangement has been described as 'a team of clergy ministering to a group of parishes'.[1] That description would also apply, though in a different way, to the diocesan ministry team which would be available to each deanery in this strategy. The early Lincoln and Norwich groups were widely regarded as successful in bringing renewed vitality to the churches in some of the smallest communities in England. But reduction of numbers under Sheffield has left some of the clergy teams with just one man, who has thus become once again the parish priest endeavouring to keep in contact with his widely scattered flock. The only recourse is to begin again with fresh teams, but this time not restricted to stipendiary clergy. Many teams up and down the country are now being thought of in terms of shared ministry including readers, elders, non-stipendiary priests, deaconesses and lay workers. Operationally speaking this is a much more difficult exercise, although it is attractive because it is a conservative approach to shared ministry. By contrast this strategy advocates collaboration between two types of team: the diocesan ministry team and the local leadership team, with the latter being responsible for the development of mission and the former acting in a supporting role.

236.   On 22nd October 1982 the *Church Times* published a letter from two lay representatives on an East Midlands deanery synod. Their parish is part of a team ministry comprising three town and three village parishes. They wrote in the following terms:

'We are becoming increasingly frustrated by the role of the deanery synod here... In many ways the Team acts as a mini-deanery synod, and it is becoming increasingly clear that both organisations have severely limited functions... As the number of team and group ministries grow, the time must surely come when the role of the deanery synod in the synodical system should be reviewed.'

This letter takes us back to a problem which was noted in Chapter 3. Teams and groups have come into existence primarily as a means of sharing resources beyond parochial boundaries. This does not necessarily conflict with the strictly synodical functions of a deanery, although the existence of one strong team or group in a small deanery can affect considerably the agenda and decisions of the synod. Nevertheless those who wish to extend the collaborative approach to ministry for which teams and groups are designed inevitably see an increasingly restricted future for deaneries, and it is fair to ask whether it is possible to avoid multiplying the levels of church debate.

237.   The simplest answer is to see deaneries as group ministries. In Chapter 9 the case has been argued for making deaneries correspond to the areas in which the local Church needs to co-operate in mission if it is to relate to other ways in which the community is actually structured.[2] It has been acknowledged that this would mean a wide variation in the size of deaneries whether considered geographically, or in terms of the population or the number of parishes involved. This would be one way of expressing the local Church, a way integrally related to the public congregations in the parishes, and to the project and work cells in which groups of Christians worked together in specific areas of action. Two consequences for the synodical processes should be noted. One is that the suitability of electing diocesan and general synod members through voting in deanery synods would become more apparent than it is sometimes felt to be at present. The other point is that matters referred for debate from diocesan synods would not be taken both to deanery synods and to PCCs. If the matter was concerned with mission, for example, it would be discussed in the deanery; if with worship, in the parish. It would also be part of the activity of the deanery to mount occasional public meetings on major issues. The deployment of diocesan ministry teams would take place through the deanery, and support of the stipendiary ministry would be by means of a deanery quota. In all this the essential point would be to see the local Church as variously arranged in deanery, congregation and cell, and by these means engaged in complementary rather than separate activities.

238.   For the immediate future it appears that most progress with church unity is likely to take place at local level, and especially through the development of local ecumenical projects (LEPs), although the significance of agreed 'faith and order' statements will also be considerable and it is not impossible that some form of covenanting may yet win acceptance at a national level. One particular result of a theological basis for agreement on ministry and the sacraments being achieved (in response to ARCIC and the Lima Text) would be a much fuller development of LEPs than is possible at present. If deaneries are to correspond to areas where local congregations need to be sharing resources and co-operating in mission, as this strategy suggests that they should, then it would follow that entire deaneries ought to be involved in LEPs: indeed, the definition of the deanery in these instances would be a local ecumenical Church, and the deanery mission committee would be a fully ecumenical body even though some individual congregations in the deanery would retain distinctive forms of worship and other marks of their own denominational inheritance.[3] The real problem to be faced in such an extension of local ecumenical commitment would not, however, lie in the area of differing traditions of worship so much as in different approaches to mission. This has already been found to be particularly acute, for example, in co-operation with the black-led, independent and pentecostal churches which exist in urban priority areas.[4]

DIOCESAN STRATEGIES

239.   It was noted in Chapter 2 that the 1978 policy document from the House of Bishops entitled *The Future of the Ministry* (GS 374) called upon every diocese to consider 'its responsibility for recruiting, training and developing the forms of ministry which the Church will need in the next twenty-five years'. The need to consider the most effective deployment of the Sheffield allocation of stipendiary clergy has also prompted dioceses to develop more specific strategies. This has been done in some cases through diocesan pastoral committees in consultation with deaneries. In a number of dioceses working parties have been set up to take an overall look at strategy, and this has led or will eventually lead to debate in the diocesan synod. One report which has already been debated is *Models for the Eighties–Strategies for Mission and Pastoral Care in the Diocese of Guildford*. This has sought to take account of the differing needs of various types of community to be found within the diocese, viz. town centres, commuter-farming villages, urban-housing areas of high density, suburban housing areas of medium-low density, and extra-parochial communities and areas of pastoral care. A different strategy is proposed for each area.[5]

240.   An exercise of this type in every diocese would be rendered more rather than less necessary by the adoption of a national strategy of the kind proposed in this study. To determine the requirements of different

communities in a remote, centralised way would be unworkable. The chapters on rural and urban ministry have been included here to supply some general 'earthing' to the analysis of the existing situation. The strategy itself does not pretend to provide detailed solutions. In a far more comprehensive way than is possible under the present system of appointments the Bishop would have to make decisions about the best use of the diocesan ministry teams according to the varying needs and opportunities of each locality. His other responsibility would be to encourage each local Church to become aware of its own resources for its mission. A board of ministry.and officers for ministry would be needed to formulate policy, advise the Bishop, and share his tasks of consultation with local Churches and of training and developing the various forms of ministry required.

241. We have already considered the need for the office of Bishop itself to be exercised corporately. Dioceses should have freedom to work out the best pattern for themselves. Three basic alternative patterns of episcopal ministry suggest themselves. Some dioceses have a natural focus where the cathedral is situated in an urban centre: they are similar to the primitive episcopate where the diocesan was situated in the cathedral city with one or more suffragans *(chorepiskopoi)* exercising oversight in the surrounding area. Other dioceses cover more than one area of local government and social organisation and in these an area system is clearly appropriate. Thirdly, there are dioceses which equate to a single area of local government, where a collegial approach may be better. Dioceses which neither have a natural centre nor are coterminous with one or more areas of local government probably need to have their boundaries revised.

242. Major responsibilities would thus belong to the diocese as well as to each local Church in future strategy. We must now turn to consider the implications for selection and training, which at present involve regulations and procedures which are agreed at national level.

NOTES TO CHAPTER 17: WAYS OF STRUCTURING MINISTRY

[1]Cf. A. Russell, *Collaborative Ministry in the Countryside*, An unpublished working paper, 1983.

[2]Cf. the recommendation of the Partners in Mission Consultation:
'Greater use should be made of the deanery level for co-operative training and mission. The deanery is probably also the best level for ecumenical co-operation and relationships with municipal bodies.' (*PIM Report*, p.39, para.152)

[3]An example of a development along these lines, although not on the scale of a whole deanery, is described in Tap Roots, No.3: *Sherborne Ecumenical Parish*, BCC. See also the diagram in Appendix 3.

[4]See e.g. *A Parish for a Modern City: Southampton Team Ministry 1973-1982*, p.26: 'For ourselves, we do not see it as part of our task to "convert" people of other faiths... Our difficulties arise when those Christian brothers who are identified with us through their use of our halls choose to operate a directly evangelistic approach which runs counter to the way in which we have been working in the area, and which could seriously jeopardise our own relationships with the local people.'

[5]See also *Appropriate Patterns: An Integrated Strategy for Readers, NSMs and LNSMs*, by a Working Party of the Bishop's Advisory Council on Ministry, Diocese of Birmingham, 1983.

# 18: Calling

243.   The development of shared ministry in the Church, when it is related to mission, results in a change of emphasis from recruitment of a trained body of 'professionals' to call-up for active service by every baptised member. Just as the army today maintains its strength by urging young people to consider military service as a fulfilling career, so there has been a tendency in the Church to encourage individuals to consider the possibility of a call to full-time service. But the circumstances of the Church's mission are closer to the analogy of the last war, when it was necessary for all able-bodied individuals to be involved. There is a further similarity as well, because although we may be ready and willing enough to respond to the need, and desire with all our hearts to be of service, the 'call-up' and the 'posting' must still come from outside ourselves. Thus the Church must discern and confirm the particular vocation of each 'faithful soldier and servant' of Christ.

SELECTION FOR ORDAINED MINISTRY

244.   The existence of a general 'call-up' for ministry therefore by no means excludes the specific vocation to serve Christ in the public and representative ministries of his Church which are signified by orders. It does, however, raise the question of what is the distinctive character of such a vocation. This has been the subject of a recent report on selection criteria produced by a working group of the Candidates' Committee of ACCM, which is due to be published during 1983 as an ACCM Occasional Paper.[1] The work has been done in conjunction with a revision of the Selectors' Handbook, and is therefore related to the existing situation in which national conferences are arranged to assess the vocations of candidates for the following categories of ministry:

| | |
|---|---|
| ordained stipendiary | stipendiary deaconess |
| ordained non-stipendiary | non-stipendiary deaconess |
| ordained local non-stipendiary | stipendiary lay worker |
| | non-stipendiary lay worker |

In practice these two columns correspond to the division between male and female candidates, although there is nothing to prevent a man from offering for ministry as an accredited lay worker. (There are of course men serving in accredited lay ministry, both as readers and as Church Army captains, but these have separate processes of selection in which ACCM is not involved.) If the present proposals for the admission of women to the Order of Deacon are implemented, then in future there may be men and women offering for a distinctively diaconal ministry in place of the present all-female order. Whether in those circumstances the category of licensed lay worker would continue is not yet known.

245.   The selection criteria report uses the term 'professional ministries' to cover all the categories listed above, thus signifying that what is envisaged in each case is a public, representative ministry authorised by the Church as a whole, which bears certain expectations on the part of society and receives appropriate training for this purpose. (It is on this distinctive basis that it is possible to consider the existence of a particular vocation to be a non-stipendiary lay worker, which might otherwise seem to represent a base-line of commitment for every Christian.)

246.   The strategy here presented, however, would alter the list of categories currently subject to national selection and authorisation. It is suggested that 'professional ministry' in the sense just defined should correspond to 'ordained ministry' alone. Note that this does not imply either greater proficiency, higher status or superior training, all of which may be associated in common speech with the word 'professional'. The selection criteria report has to use the word because none other is available to indicate the particular relationship between the individual and the institution he or she represents which is at present borne both by the ordained and by the nationally selected and accredited lay ministry. In the terms of this strategy this would no longer apply, because such a relationship would be confined to bishops, priests and deacons. Candidates for national selection would therefore all be offering for ordained ministry.

247.   Furthermore, at the stage of selection no final distinction would need to be made between those who would serve as deacons and those who would be ordained to the priesthood (except, of course, for women so long as they are not admitted to the priesthood). One interesting feature of the selection criteria report is that it devotes by far the greater amount of space to a discussion of the criteria relating to candidates for all types of 'professional' ministry and proportionately much less to distinguishing between the distinctive qualities of each particular vocation. The point is that when it comes to assessing those who have a calling to serve the Church in a public and representative way there are important qualities of faith, spirituality, personality, relationships and intelligence which are to be looked for in *all* candidates. Since it is the task of the Bishops' Selectors to recommend for training, not for ordination, it appears possible that a future strategy could include selection conferences which were concerned solely with this common area of investigation.[2]

248.   The selection process would then have two further stages. One would be continuing assessment during training, through which the relationship of an individual's gifts to their expression in either diaconal or priestly ministry

would be clarified. The final stage would be job selection for a place in a diocesan ministry team. This would involve a judgment about how these gifts could best be exercised in the context of a particular ministerial appointment. This final stage would of course be repeated in each subsequent appointment for which a minister was considered. Each time there would be interviews on the basis of a job description.[3]

SELECTION FOR NON-STIPENDIARY MINISTRY

249.    An important issue to be resolved is at which stage the question of stipendiary or non-stipendiary ministry should be settled. At present it is usually clear from the start that a candidate is only prepared to consider one or the other; but the strategy has raised the question of whether it is right to think in terms of separate vocations, and in any case the evidence of the NSM report shows that a considerable amount of transfer in both directions is going on. My proposal therefore is that candidates should offer simply for ordination. In the case of those who have not finished their higher education at the time of the conference, and of those who are unemployed, the assumption would no doubt be that if ordained they would be maintained in their ministry by the Church. For others it could be argued that the question of stipendiary or non-stipendiary is only relevant to particular appointments and should therefore be left until the final stage of selection is reached. There are, however, obvious practical difficulties in doing so. If a candidate is to have any residential training this will require in most cases leaving existing employment. Even if a candidate is trained entirely by means of a part-time course the fact of preparing for ordination will cause unsettlement both at home and also at work so long as it is not decided whether this will mean a change of job, home and education for the children. It will not be possible to make plans, and career prospects may be jeopardised.

250.    In the next chapter it will be suggested that all training for ordained ministry should begin with an initial period during which connections could be explored between the ordinand's sense of vocation and his or her existing occupation. If there appeared to be a clear calling to a ministry as deacon or priest in that situation then the candidate would eventually join a diocesan ministry team in a non-stipendiary capacity, and a decision would be made about this at the end of the vocational assessment year. These remarks of course apply to what is currently understood by a work-based non-stipendiary ministry. The selection criteria report also notes the occurrence of NSM candidates who are primarily interested in a parish-based ministry, either as an 'auxiliary' to an incumbent or following retirement from a secular job. This strategy regards such people as candidates for local ministry, and selection for this must now be considered.

SELECTION FOR LOCAL ORDAINED MINISTRY

251.    Deacons and priests are ordained to work in the Church of God, and the particular sphere of their ministry is defined by the Bishop's licence. In

practice of course it is also limited by divisions between the churches, but in principle ordination signifies a relationship to the whole people of God, not merely to one congregation. There can be no abandonment of this practice without creating two types of orders. But one implication of this strategy is that congregations do not have to wait for the 'Church of God' out there somewhere to send them a deacon or a priest: they *are* the Church of God called to ministry in that place, and can therefore put forward their own candidates, if it also seems good to the Holy Spirit. That essential condition is tested by taking into account the mind of the wider Church.

252.   This much is common ground in current thinking about local ordained ministry in the Church of England, but two alternative ways of making this reference have been proposed. The one which has so far been the practice laid down by the Bishops' regulations for selection and training is that all candidates for local ministry should attend national selection conferences, but a diocesan representative should in each case be available to inform the Selectors, not about the candidate, but about the context in which it is proposed that this ministry should be exercised.

253.   Another procedure has been suggested which would make use of experienced Selectors from other dioceses in an assessment which would take place within the candidates' own diocese, or every deanery. The difference between these two approaches reflects on the one hand a desire not to allow the local support for a candidate to predetermine the outcome of the enquiry; and on the other, an anxiety that a local candidate, if removed from his own situation and summoned to a national conference, will be measured against some yardstick appropriate to the stipendiary ministry in the interests of 'maintaining standards'.

254.   Reference to what has been said in Chapter 15 will show that the strategy envisages that as leaders emerge in the local Church they would be called into the eldership team without ordination being considered at that stage. If they were later to be put forward as candidates for ordination a negative response from a selection conference would certainly not reverse the calling to them to exercise lay leadership in the local Church, any more than readers or churchwardens who have a vocation to the priesthood tested on a selection conference at present would automatically cease to be readers or churchwardens if they were not recommended to train for ordination. The calling from the local Church is to join the corporate leadership of shared ministry in that place; for their part the Selectors would consider only those essential qualities which must be found in all who are to be called upon to bear the wider significance of the Church's ordained ministry. These qualities remain the same, whatever differences in training and in function there might be between diocesan and local priests. For these reasons it would seem right to insist that all candidates for ordination should attend the

same national selection procedure, while granting that the criteria to be used in it should be limited to those which may properly be applied to all candidates.

## WHAT ABOUT VOCATIONS TO ACCREDITED LAY MINISTRY?

255.   In the terms of this strategy it has been suggested that a nationally accredited lay ministry should cease to exist. But what should be done if vocations to such a ministry persist? There are perhaps two aspects to a desire that the Church should affirm lay ministry by recognising its contribution alongside ordained ministry. The first is to acknowledge the existence of a specifically lay vocation. This, I have tried to show in Chapter 8, is to adopt a negative attitude to lay ministry by showing that it is right for some people *not* to be ordained. Theologically there is no such thing as lay ministry: there is only the ministry of the laity within which the various ministries (including ordained ministry) find their place. It is natural enough, at a time when the Church is rediscovering the existence of other ministries apart from orders, for there to be a desire for their value to be recognised. But the way to affirm lay vocations is to make their basis in baptism more explicit.

256.   There is, however, a second aspect to this which seems to be present in many of the candidates who are now coming forward for accredited lay ministry. They wish to offer some particular professional skill in such a way that they may be seen to be making the contribution of the Church's ministry alongside colleagues who work for secular caring agencies. This is most important, but I have tried to suggest in Chapter 14 that it is rightly seen as part of the Church's *diakonia* to the community. They should therefore be candidates for the diaconate, and it is interesting to note that at the present time the great majority of those offering for accredited lay ministry are deaconess candidates. If they all become deacons in due course, as seems likely, the number of licensed lay workers will soon become quite small. I believe that these ministers should either be encouraged to enter the diaconate or be accepted as lay pastors within the leadership of their local churches.

### NOTES TO CHAPTER 18: CALLING

[1] *Selection for Ministry: A Report on Criteria*, ACCM Occasional Paper No.12, 1983.
[2] The area is clearly defined in the selection criteria report. In the draft text it occupies twenty-one pages of typescript compared with two or three pages each on the distinctive qualities necessary for ordained stipendiary, non-stipendiary, and accredited lay ministry.
[3] See the diagram in Appendix 4 for a summary of the various stages of selection, assessment and training for ordained ministry envisaged in Chapters 18 and 19.

# 19: Equipment

257.   The development of shared ministry implies a need, and indeed stimulates a demand, for lay training. Already the growth of lay training schemes has been such that there is a danger of losing the distinction between training for ministry and the provision of Christian education. Just as 'ministry' has become a greedy concept, threatening to expand until it covers all Christian activity, so the whole purpose of learning in the Church is liable to become related to preparation for engaging in some form of ministry. That is far too narrow an understanding of the Church's interest in education. At the other extreme, it must be admitted, there are some equally unsatisfactory definitions of Christian education which are indistinguishable from humanist ones. The distinctive aim of Christian education is for wholeness in Christ, with all that that implies both for personal maturity and for living in community. Although it is sometimes difficult to draw a precise line between a broader-based educational programme and a ministry training scheme, the latter should in principle be designed as an element in the former. There is an important area here for co-operation between education and ministry 'specialists', both within dioceses and at the national level.

258.   Education is also a subject of relevance *within* the training schemes, particularly for those whose ministry involves a call to teach. How education takes place in the Church, and how people learn, are vast subjects which this study is unable to deal with adequately. Debates which are going on at present on these matters will undoubtedly have an influence on future patterns.[1] Our concern here must be with the training implications of the strategy, and the most obvious of these is the provision of ministerial training for the laity. At present about ten dioceses have developed Bishop's Certificate courses, which may or may not be regarded as giving a kind of basic qualification for lay ministry. The diocese of Birmingham is producing study courses related to an initial report concerned with education and training for lay ministry.[2] The diocese of St Albans has a ministerial training scheme which prepares people together for ordination, accredited lay ministry, and other kinds of lay leadership. Few of these schemes have yet reckoned fully with a movement known as Theological Education by Extension (TEE) which originated in Latin America and has spread rapidly, especially to areas where church growth has produced an acute problem of a shortage of ordained ministers. TEE sets out to make theological resources

145

available to the whole Church by means of 'distance-learning' methods, and so to release the ministry of the laity.[3]

259. The Church of England certainly has much to learn from TEE, although its application is likely to be most effective if it is made regionally and ecumenically rather than nationally.[4] In what follows I wish to explore the possibilities of introducing a clear distinction between training which is seen as preparation for general Christian witness, and more specific kinds of ministerial development.

AN AGREED CURRICULUM

260. In every place something is needed which will be adequate 'to prepare all God's people for the work of Christian service' (Ephesians 4.12 GNB). For this purpose it would be possible to suggest a nationally recognised general training scheme. But this idea has several disadvantages. It would be too inflexible to take into account the varieties of local ministry; it would not easily allow for some of the realities of adult education, which require a starting-point based in experience, and a degree of spontaneity to meet the questions which people begin to ask only after something has happened; it would also be likely to produce a sizeable administrative structure. Most serious of all would be the danger that such a 'foundation course' would be regarded as a stepping-stone to training for some more specific form of Christian ministry, whereas its most important contribution would be to encourage a developing lay consciousness that all baptised Christians already have a ministry in their daily environment which can be strengthened through training.

261. For these reasons it is better to think in terms of general training continuing to be provided through local courses, some parish-based, some deanery-based, and some diocesan-based according to the availability of resources. There would, however, be great benefits if it proved possible to devise some agreed curriculum to which all such general training might relate. Its object would be to define those things which any Christian needs to grasp in order to gain a grounding in the faith and an awareness of the contemporary context of the Church's witness. It would influence local training courses in preparing the laity, not so much to undertake ministry within the Church as to face the hard issues which confront their faith in the modern world. Clearly the catechism goes only part of the way to meeting this.

262. The existence of such a curriculum would have a practical advantage in the present stage of development in information technology, because it would be a useful stimulus to the production of sophisticated and very expensive teaching materials, the creation of which is delayed unless their potential market is clearly identified. For those called to specialist ministries

146

it would also ensure that resources and time would not be wasted in their later training by filling in gaps. The importance of this is made abundantly clear through the present selection and training procedures for accredited ministry, whether lay or ordained. Many candidates attend selection conferences and begin training with hardly more than a minimal understanding of the Christian faith, little knowledge of the Bible, and a confused approach to moral questions. Valuable and expensive training time is consequently spent covering basic matters.

263. The curriculum should also be designed to help those who are thinking about their vocation to explore their experience of God and their self-understanding before committing themselves to a more specific form of training. It is true that the reflective opportunities provided by the learning process are helpful in clarifying a vocation, but it is better if these occur in a context which arouses no particular expectations. This seems to be a disadvantage of allowing people to begin a course which is recognised for ordination training before they are clear about their own commitment.

ORDINATION TRAINING

264. Preparation for ordained ministry would take place in three stages.[5] Following recommendation by the Selectors all candidates for ordination as diocesan deacons or priests would spend one year of further vocational assessment. For those who were in higher education or unemployed at the time of their selection this first year could be spent attached to a diocesan ministry team and related to the training institution which would receive them at the end of this period: it would be, in effect, an initial placement. For those in employment at the time of their selection the year would be important as a means of exploring their aptitudes in ministry through their attempting a number of part-time projects. At the end of this first year all candidates would write a self-assessment which would form the basis of decisions about diaconal or priestly, stipendiary or non-stipendiary ministry in line with what was suggested in the previous chapter. It would also be open to those advising on the assessment to recommend either a further year to be spent on the same basis (as in the present requirements of the Aston Training Scheme) or that a candidate should not proceed.

265. Further training before ordination would then consist of two years' full-time or three years' part-time preparation.[6] The emphasis of this second stage would be upon development of an integrated theology using study of the Bible, history and the behavioural sciences together with reflection upon previous experience. The basis of this integrated course would be the relationship between prayer, belief and action in the mission of the Church. This may be expressed in diagrammatic form as follows:

Worship (Prayer) — MISSION — Doctrine (Belief) — Ethics — Pastoralia (Action) — Liturgy — Spirituality

The relationship of this course to the preceding and following stages would constitute distinctive ordination training, but otherwise the course would be available as a theological resource for lay training as well. Much the same would apply to the part-time courses, although a different experience of community and an alternative way of 'doing theology' have already become characteristic features of these.

266.   For some candidates the preliminary year of assessment would be incorporated at the expense of some reduction in residential training, since present regulations prescribe *three* years in college for those under thirty. On the other hand, the content of the two-year course would be significantly reduced from existing requirements, especially in the area of pastoral studies. The latter has recently been summarised under five heads:

 i) The input of various areas of knowledge.
 ii) The learning of certain skills.
 iii) Exposure to life in society.
 iv) Experience of life in the Christian fellowship.
 v) Supervised practical experience.[7]

Most of this would be redistributed to the earlier or later stages of training, leaving pastoral theology as part of the two-year curriculum.

267.   At the end of this second stage ordination would take place. The link between the diaconate and the priesthood, which requires priestly ministry to be undertaken as part of Christ's own lowly service to his brothers and sisters, must be clearly expressed. But a distinctive diaconate will only be confused by the continued existence of deacons who are trainee priests. It would therefore be preferable, in place of their year as a deacon, to include the call to diaconal ministry for priests within the first part of their ordination service.

268.   The new diocesan deacons and priests would become members of diocesan ministry teams and now the third stage, their induction training, would begin.[8] It would be related to a particular context and type of ministry, because all diocesan ministers would be 'specialists' according to their individual gifts. Thus for example a newly-ordained deacon or priest joining a diocesan ministry team in a rural area would receive appropriate training in that context, which is difficult to provide at present, when few

training parishes exist in rural areas. And this process of training on the job would be repeated over and over again, because further selection (not of course for ordination, but for a particular job) and appropriate induction training would be necessary at each future change in the type of ministry being undertaken. This is one aspect of in-service training, the broad lines of which would correspond to the recommendations which have already been approved as set out in *The Continuing Education of the Church's Ministers* (GS Misc. 122). Induction into each job would be supplemented by refreshment within it, on the principle of no ministering without continuing learning.

TRAINING FOR LOCAL MINISTRY

269. To support the different ministries needed in each local Church specific training courses would have to be available in each diocese to equip people for evangelism and personal witness, for preaching and teaching, for leading groups, for counselling and other aspects of pastoral work, for enabling worship, for church administration and for leadership. Any such courses, since they are related to specific forms of ministry, would assume coverage of the general curriculum first and be built on to this in the same way as ordination training. The diocese of Lichfield is already devising training units which can be arranged into a pattern along these lines.[9]

270. Those who are put forward and selected for a local ordained ministry would participate in one of the part-time courses which are recognised for ordination training. For them, the initial year of vocational assessment suggested for diocesan ordinands would not be necessary since this would already have been tested through their previous training with, and membership of, a local eldership team. The use made by the candidate for local ordained ministry of the three year part-time theological course, and the ingredients of the post-ordination induction training, would have to be worked out in relation to the context of each community and the availability of other local ministers in each place. The concept of 'appropriate training' is more useful than variation of standards in this regard, but there is no question that an effective local ministry would need the stimulation of a training for its ordained ministry which was carried out alongside candidates from other places through the present type of recognised part-time course, demanding though this would be. If this prevented many local churches from finding a candidate for the priesthood at first, that would be one good reason for continuing to make the ministry of diocesan priests available to them. For those who do acquire a local priest or deacon by these means it must be made clear that those so ordained, though bearing fully the representative ministry of orders, have actually been trained for that particular local ministry alone. If they subsequently move to another place, no new local ministry is likely to be possible without further 'appropriate training' both in the relevant theological groundwork and in perception of that local community and its ministerial needs.

271.   By comparison with the existing situation the strategy would place much greater emphasis upon team ministry, and all training must therefore take this into account. Many ordinands will begin their preparation by joining a diocesan ministry team; the final stage of induction training will occur after they have taken their places as deacons and priests on such a team. The intervening stage of theological education therefore requires a community in which the norms are corporate decision-making, shared responsibilities and joint action. The teaching work should be done on a collaborative basis, not only because the nature of applied theology requires integrated studies, but also because the method of teaching will be highly formative for the style of ministry which results from the teaching programme.

272.   Shared ministry involves ordained and lay ministers in working together: there will need to be opportunities for learning together. The training institutions can draw on the international development of TEE to devise ways of making theological study available to the laity. In Britain over the next forty years this will perhaps take the form of programmed learning taking advantage of developments in technology and using the Open University model. There should be no elitism about the training provided for the Church's ordained ministers, but it is right to continue to look to them for considerable theological resources in support of the local Church's mission. During induction training for particular appointments it will be vital for deacons, priests and lay pastors to work together to produce an applied theology in a given context.

USE OF THE CHURCH'S TRAINING INSTITUTIONS

273.   It is desirable that the training institutions should be involved in providing much wider resources than are required for pre-ordination training alone. In the colleges there is a concentration of library and administrative facilities and residential capacity which can be used for lay training and for clergy in-service training. Both the colleges and the courses can develop effective programmes of extension studies and assist the co-ordination of training throughout a particular region. But in order to do these things their staffing will have to be put on a different footing from the present ratio which is limited to numbers of students in residence or enrolled for the pre-ordination course.

TRAINING FOR MINISTRY IN AN URBAN AND PLURALISTIC SOCIETY

274.   Finally we must go back to the chapters exploring the situation within which the Church's strategy for ministry has to be developed. We have noted there the emphatically urban and pluralistic nature of British society as a whole as it nears the end of the twentieth century. A recent survey of training for industrial ministry has concluded as follows:

'It would seem that there is still a reluctance to recognise, in training, any other field than the local church/parish/circuit situation. More module training, taking into account the complexities of modern urban industrial society, ought perhaps at least to be included in the final year of all training for ministry in contemporary society.'[10]

275. The strategy offers the possibility of structuring ministry in ways which are more responsive to the demands of mission to such a society. The training must therefore reflect this, and in this strategy a two-fold approach is proposed. It is suggested that it will be important, but no more than partially adequate, to ensure that the colleges and courses are geared to producing ministers who are socially aware and responsible.[11] There must also be, in addition to that, an element which is built into the post-ordination induction training: this will be designed to explore the relevance of each particular diocesan appointment to the growth of socially aware and responsible local churches. Few things are more important for the future of the Church's mission than educational programmes which will overcome the gap at present so evident between the concerns of 'specialist' ministers and the preoccupations of many local congregations. Proposals for training ordinands to minister in an urban and pluralistic society, if they are limited to what is to be supplied prior to ordination, will result only in ministry with a blunted edge, because it is impossible at that stage to experience the complexity of 'world-in-church' and 'church-in-world' with which we were concerned in earlier chapters.

NOTES TO CHAPTER 19: EQUIPMENT

[1]Of relevance here are: *The Child in the Church*, BCC, 1976; D. Gillett, *How Do Congregations Learn?*, Grove Booklet on Ministry and Worship No.67, Grove Books, 1979; *Learning and Teaching in Theological Education*, ACCM Occasional Paper No.11, issued in conjunction with the Board of Education of the General Synod, 1982; *The Continuing Education of the Church's Ministers*, GS Misc. 122, 1980, p.13f.

[2]See *Power to the People of God*, a report of the Advisory Council for Training of the Diocese of Birmingham, 1981.

[3]See *Ministry by the People: Theological Education by Extension*, ed. F. R. Kinsler, WCC Publications, Geneva and Orbis Books, Maryknoll, 1983.

[4]Cf. *Alternative Patterns of Training*, GS 265, 1975; *Theological Training: A Policy for the Future*, A Report by the House of Bishops, GS 303, 1976; *Theological Training: A Policy for the Future*, The Guildford Report, GS Misc. 57, 1977.

[5]See the diagram in Appendix 4 for a summary of the various stages of selection, assessment and training for ordained ministry envisaged in Chapters 18 and 19.

[6]The exceptions to this general rule would be:
(i) theology graduates who might be required to have no more than one year in full-time training (the arguments against the wisdom of this would have been met by the initial year's placement – cf. *The Second Report of the Working Party on Courses*, GS 359, 1977, pp.19–22); and
(ii) candidates who were recommended at the end of the vocational assessment year to attempt a theology degree.

[7]See M. Wharton, 'Pastoral studies in an Anglican theological college', in *Contact. the Interdisciplinary Journal of Pastoral Studies*, No.78, 1983, pp.9–13.

[8]A great deal of the material in *The Training of Training Incumbents*, ACCM Occasional Paper No.10, 1982, would remain relevant despite the disappearance of incumbents.

[9]*On Patterns of Ministry:* The Report of the Ministry Working Party to the Bishop's Council, Diocese of Lichfield, 1980.

[10]T. Elwyn, *Theological Training for Industrial Ministry*, The Churches' Consortium on Industrial Mission, Recommended Paper Four, 1980, p.14.

[11]The present contribution of the training institutions to preparing candidates for ministry in a multi-faith society has been assessed by Kenneth Cracknell of the BCC, in a paper entitled *Theological Education in a Multi-Faith Society*, 1981.

# THE WAY FORWARD

# 20: Alternatives

276. The picture which has been drawn in this strategy of the Church of England as it might be organised for its mission in the twenty-first century may appear to many of its present members as strange and disturbing. Yet it is possible to demonstrate that no developments are here proposed which are not already beginning or under active consideration. I noted in the Introduction that the Partners-in-Mission Consultation in 1981 identified the growth of shared ministry as a key issue for the future. This affects every church member, and is complementary to the increasing practice of a collaborative approach to the ordained and accredited ministries of the Church. Diocesan specialist teams already exist, as do elders exercising corporate leadership in local churches. A vital and active order of deacons has been called for; readers have begun to undertake a more pastoral role; a local ordained ministry is planned and even beginning to appear in several dioceses; non-stipendiary priests are exploring opportunities for mission outside the parochial system.

277. At the moment it is directly against agreed policy to suggest abandoning the attempt to staff the parishes with stipendiary clergy, and indeed most of the new forms of ministry just referred to have been accepted on the understanding that they will work in close conjunction with, and mostly under the supervision of, the full-time parochial clergy. My proposal to abolish the position of the incumbent, although not by any means a new idea, is therefore the one point in the strategy which could be said to go against present developments. However, I shall argue in a moment that the breakdown of the parochial system, because of the impossible demands that are now being made on the beneficed clergy, is in practice the real development which is taking place, whatever the agreed policy may be.

278. So the ingredients of my strategy are already, for the most part, present in the contemporary Church and are bound to develop in one direction or another. But these developments might very easily occur in different, and mutually incompatible, directions. It is for this reason that I believe the Advisory Council for the Church's Ministry has been right to judge that the Church is now in need of a national strategy for its ministry. This need might in other circumstances be questioned and indeed even now it is important to respect the necessary limits of any national strategy. Each diocese, and each local Church, has its proper area of freedom and corresponding responsibility to develop a ministry which matches the varying

155

opportunities for mission in accordance with the guidance of the Holy Spirit. I hope that these freedoms have been safeguarded in my proposals, so that the effect would be a liberation of ministry from all unnecessarily restrictive structures.

279. The strategy is therefore an attempt to relate what seem to be vigorous signs of growth in the Church's ministry to a coherent programme for mission by the people of God and Christian nurture within the community. Without this there are serious possibilities of confusion, for example between what is intended by a local priesthood, an eldership, and a permanent diaconate. Within the presbyterate, catholic order could be turned into the disorder of quite distinct and separate priesthoods.

280. On the particular matter of a local ordained ministry my observation is that exciting developments are beginning, but that on the whole the Church is looking for candidates in the wrong places. If this ministry is limited to the small congregations of the inner city and the deep countryside it is unlikely to flourish as a truly enabling resource for the Body of Christ; it could become part of a largely paper strategy for filling in the gaps left by the stipendiary clergy, and succeed only in theory. In my view the true starting point for local ordained ministry must be where the Church is already growing in faith as well as numbers and lay Christians are reaching maturity. The strategy has made this one of the strong reasons for more co-operation in mission within deaneries, since many deaneries will have both stronger and weaker parishes.

A STRATEGY WHICH ACCEPTS THE CHURCH'S PRESENT SITUATION

281. A case can therefore be made out for claiming that it is now a priority for the Church to come to some agreement about a future strategy. It is clear that such a strategy will be most useful if it brings into some sort of constructive relationship the different kinds of ministry which are now apparent. I have also considered it important to set this strategy in the context of contemporary social change, and to pay serious attention to the lessons which can be learned from the history of the Church's ministry during the past twenty years. Those were my concerns in the first four chapters, and in particular I have tried to reckon with the four conclusions of Chapter 2 in my proposals. I do not think any alternative strategy could be either realistic or credible if it did not take account of those conclusions.

ALTERNATIVE 1–MORE FULL-TIME PARISH PRIESTS

282. What are the alternatives? It is true that since 1978 the Church of England has had a partial strategy for its ministry, when it adopted a target for ordination candidates in order to continue to maintain a nationwide parochial ministry. This is only a partial strategy, because there is no more

than a passing reference in the agreed policy document to 'the development of a variety of ministries'. I have already shown that the strategy of setting a recruitment target for stipendiary ordained ministers is not working, and therefore, if the Church wishes to pursue this strategy, it must put far more resources and effort into it than it is prepared to do at present. So far, the increase that has occurred in the number of ordinands in training has resulted in anxiety about increasing costs. I accept that this has generally expressed itself in terms of proper questions about whether the money is being well spent, but the conclusion of a working party set up to look into this has been that most improvements in training are likely to cost more rather than less than the present comparatively modest amount which the Church spends on the training of its ministers.[1] Again, a strategy which depends on recruitment is unlikely to succeed unless much more recruitment is actually attempted. I discern little enthusiasm at present for sizeable budgets to be spent on publicity, or for setting apart a Sunday to focus on vocations, or even to make more of the ember seasons. There can of course be no direct correlation between the amount spent on publicising the need for more priests and the number of candidates coming forward: vocations depend much more upon the atmosphere which the Church breathes than upon the resources it invests. Nevertheless, if the Church wishes to base its strategy on a generous supply of priests being available, then it must say so clearly and frequently. The truth is that the Church is not at present uniformly enthusiastic about this approach; but enthusiasm there must be if the parishes are going to be staffed adequately on the traditional basis. Even if the total number of parochial clergy has now almost reached its lowest point and we are able to look forward to some modest increase by the end of the century, which is the present hope, this is not really anything like enough. It is an observable fact that in many places the parochial system, as an effective means of mission and pastoral care available to all, has already in large measure broken down.

ALTERNATIVE 2 – A COLLABORATIVE APPROACH TO PARISH MINISTRY

283.    To cope with this situation it would be possible to propose a development of shared ministry involving NSMs (where available) as auxiliary pastoral ministers, women deacons in the same role but without authorisation to preside at the Eucharist, and a fuller use of lay ministry to support the clergy. Where these measures were not sufficient to meet the need, as in some rural or inner-city areas, the parochial system would be replaced by the suspension of all livings and the establishment instead of stipendiary team ministries. I would be disposed to describe this approach, perhaps rather severely, as propping up the parochial system. It bears the marks of a holding operation rather than of new growth.

284.    My concern has been to suggest a strategy which is not solely addressed to dealing with the shortage of stipendiary clergy, but takes account of all the

157

conclusions reached in Chapter 2. It is a strategy for development in ministry. By contrast the alternative just described would continue to prevent the emergence of mature lay leadership, would veil the responsibilities of the local Church for undertaking its own mission, and would retain the 'general practitioner' emphasis of the parish priest. Above all, the parochial ministry would remain so dominant that very little energy could be devoted to other aspects of mission. Moreover, so long as patronage and benefices continued to exist it is likely that parishes possessing articulate and influential lay people would tend to obtain more than their fair share of the stipendiary clergy. The irony in this sort of strategy is that it is just the parishes who should be out in the lead with new forms of ministry who manage to hang on most effectively to the means of perpetuating the traditional patterns. This would not be so bad if it were not done at the expense of other, more needy areas, which is bound to be the case so long as the resources for supplying traditional ministry remain inadequate.

NOTES TO CHAPTER 20: ALTERNATIVES

[1] *The Financing of Training:* The Report of a Joint Working Party appointed by the Advisory Council for the Church's Ministry and the Central Board of Finance of the Church of England, GS Misc. 175, March 1983.

# 21: Initiatives

285.   In this concluding chapter I will take the liberty of supposing that my analysis of the present situation in the first four chapters is substantially accurate, and that I have succeeded in offering a strategy which is both coherent in itself and squarely based on the preceding analysis and existing developments in ministry. If all this were to be weighed by the Church and considered true, there remains the supreme difficulty of knowing how such a vision for the future could ever be realised. For example, I have already referred in Chapter 17 to the daunting task of removing patronage and the parson's freehold from the fabric of parochial life. The Church of England does not shed its history lightly, and I for one rejoice that this is so. I heard someone remark recently that the Church of England can be reformed only by stealth, and here I have presented a full frontal strategy. Perhaps (to improve the metaphor) it will suffer the fate of providing a smokescreen while something else is going on!

LOCAL, DIOCESAN AND NATIONAL INITIATIVES

286.   I am not, however, proposing to despair before I have finished putting pen to paper. The vitality of the laity *is* evident; the Church of England *is* receiving more candidates for ordination than most other Churches in Western Europe; the climate of opinion in this country *is* increasingly open to the influence of Christians who are prepared to live out in their own lives the claims of the Gospel, which is the true ministry of Christ. A leading national daily newspaper carried an article on 7th February 1983 which predicted that 'no revolution will ever, ever start from Church House, Westminster'. That might seem to depress the chances of a national strategy which is being offered for debate in the General Synod. But here I refer to one of the two essential ideas which were set out in Chapter 5 and developed in subsequent chapters. Acceptance of the strategy means acceptance of the principle that a great deal of responsibility rests with the local Christians in each place. That being so, the most important initiatives must come from the local Church. Without forcing the pace or attempting to construct imposing edifices of ministerial structure where the foundations are weak, dioceses should encourage local initiatives and growth wherever parishes are ready to accept the challenge. As I hope I have duly recognised, a great deal is already happening, but it is important that developments in the local Church, while expressing a proper response to local needs, should not present a confusing and inarticulate pattern. The medium of ministry is itself part of the Christian message.

159

287.   If encouragement and coherence is to be given to local initiatives there is a useful national initiative which could be taken: it would consist of a research and monitoring programme which could give guidance where it was needed, but would have as its primary purpose the spreading of information about experience with new styles of ministry; for example, local priests, leadership teams, or diaconal ministry. As each local Church contributes its own experience it becomes possible to hear what the Spirit is saying to the churches: but conversely, each local Church is also called to listen to the wider Church. This includes, of course, the Church overseas and belonging to other confessions. The missionary societies have begun to find a new role in interpreting some of that wider experience to the Church of England. They are part of the whole dimension of voluntary societies which has contributed so significantly to the witness of the Church of England in the past. Should it continue to do so? This was one of the questions considered by the Partners in Mission consultation in 1981. In the PIM report the existence of some duplication of effort, but also of much continuing vitality among the various societies was recognised, and their future contribution, perhaps in new ways and with more co-operation between themselves, was welcomed.[1] The strength of the societies is in the parishes, and a strategy which encourages local initiatives would not conflict with the PIM view of their future. However, the new emphasis of the local Church addressing itself to mission at a deanery level would indicate that the contribution of the 'home' voluntary societies might increasingly be made along specialist lines, providing experience for example in the area of youth work, or of inner-city mission, or of marriage and family life education.[2]

288.   What is to be done in those places where the local Church shows no initiative? It would be fatal for this strategy to spread by inertia; that is to say, if the parochial system with one priest possessing the cure of souls were to be replaced only where it had in effect already broken down. It is now breaking down in places where the Church is numerically weakest and under the greatest pressure. In these circumstances it is difficult to put responsibility into the hands of the local people. Responsibility belongs to them as much as in any other place, but this is not a strategy for making small groups of isolated Christians feel that the rest of the Church has deserted them. It is hardly surprising if they show few signs of taking the initiative for themselves: the Bishop, with his priests and deacons, must show the care and support of the whole diocese for them, and strengthen them to make their own witness.

289.   In one episode from Alan Bleasdale's much acclaimed BBC television series, 'The Boys from the Blackstuff', a large number of people attended the funeral of George, a greatly loved and respected community leader. The officiating priest was totally unable to connect with and articulate the feelings of George's friends. The man who attempted, by some impromptu

remarks, to supply the deeply-felt need in the congregation to mark the occasion with a true memorial was, for his part, totally unable to express the Christian hope. The scene perfectly demonstrated how the clergy must see their role in terms of enabling local people to articulate their own faith and make their own celebration.[3]

290.   There are those who would be unable to take initiatives, and there are those who would be unwilling to do so. In areas where the Church is relatively much stronger in terms of numbers and financial support it does not follow that there will be confidence and enthusiasm for a 'do-it-yourself' approach to ministry. For many loyal churchgoers it is the task of the laity to maintain the ministry of the Church by their financial contributions, and for the rest to be regular in attendance at divine worship on Sundays and to be faithful Christians in their daily lives and in saying their prayers.   They see the spiritual work of counselling souls as a very private matter for which a trained and professionally discreet person is essential. It would be a mistake to reject this attitude as lacking either in commitment or in spirituality. Its failure is rather in defining the ministry in very restrictive terms. Such members of the laity need to realise that they already possess the ingredients of a vital and positive ministry of their own. The work of personal counselling is rightly seen as one requiring specialist skills, but the future mission of the Church depends just as much and probably far more upon Christians making an active witness in society, not just as isolated individuals but consciously as the Body of Christ. The educational task in preparing the laity for ministry is not one of making all Christians into expert spiritual directors, but of delivering them from that privatised religion which is the peculiar English heresy and which fits so neatly and so dangerously into the wider privatisation of life today which was noted in the first chapter. Anyone who wishes to own the name of Christ is inescapably his ambassador.

MORE ORDINANDS

291.   I have already emphasized that it would be completely wrong to see this strategy as a way of making do with fewer clergy. In the short term the need for more priests is desperate, and nothing in the implementation of the full strategy would make the work of the ordained ministry redundant. But would people be attracted to offer themselves as candidates if the traditional role of the parish priest were abolished? Many of the clergy would say that the joy and satisfaction which they find in their work has much to do with the abundant variety of parish life. They are not likely to be enthusiastic about operating in some detached diocesan team, remote from the 'down-to-earth' problems that their present ministry brings them each day. This, however, is not the alternative as I see it. Every diocesan priest and deacon would be associated with a local Church, either in direct ministry to it, or through one of its cells operating in some particular field. He or she would in the fullest sense be a member of a local Christian community, participating in its

161

worship and witness like every other member. The clergy would continue to be involved in as much parochial ministry as at present. The essential difference is that instead of forming the 'bottlenecks' through which all ministry must flow they would become partners in an enterprise involving the contribution of each member. In making their own contribution the priests and deacons would have the opportunity to do what the rest of the laity are encouraged to do now, that is to use their gifts to glorify God according to their ability and not to attempt tasks for which they are completely unfitted. This is the true understanding of vocation. As members of diocesan teams the priests and deacons would also build those bridges between communities which is their calling in the ordained ministry but which the isolation of parish priests can so often prevent.

292.  I would hope that the future prospects for ordained ministry held out in this strategy would encourage the vocations of those who at present are frankly deterred by the unjustifiable load of expectations and even guilt carried by many of the parochial clergy. Moreover, the emphasis here given to the ministry of the laity will itself, if experience to date teaches us anything, produce further candidates for ordination, although it must not do so by creating the impression that ordination is in some way a mark of deeper commitment to Christ.

THE MINISTRY OF INTERPRETATION

293.  In this strategy I have not set out to provide all the answers. I have seen my task as one of attempting to discern some pattern in what I hear and see which would be liberating for future ministry. In putting it to paper I have understood my own ministry to be essentially one of interpretation. In closing, therefore, I draw attention to what someone else has said whose gift of interpretation has been widely recognised:

> 'If I were obliged to rough out a blueprint for the Church of the future, I would start with the need for good popular theology, to affirm that God exists and what He is like, and upon this try to effect a renewal of religious education at all ages. Next, I would drag the laity deeper and deeper into ministry of all kinds, joining lay orders, popping in and out of monasteries, preaching, healing, celebrating irregular eucharists, too, I hope. Finally, since human organisation demands leadership, we must get bishops (or moderators) back to what they were in the Celtic Church—not committee men and administrators, but evangelists and saints. I know some very holy bishops even today, but they find it hard to fit in their diaries.'[4]

I have not based my strategy on these remarks, nor am I at all points in accord with them, but they are the insights of an interpreter, and I hope that the interpreters as well as the administrators will weigh the strategy which I have presented in these pages, for whether my case is made or not, it is certain that the way forward will require a collaborative ministry of interpretation with administration.

# NOTES TO CHAPTER 21: INITIATIVES

[1] *PIM Report*, p.33, paras.115f.; GS 547, p.8, para.17.

[2] The Church Army is at present re-assessing its distinctive contribution to the mission of the Church and the House of Bishops has established a review group to assist in this process.

[3] 'George's Last Ride', an episode last broadcast on BBC1 on 8th February 1983.

[4] Gerald Priestland, 'Yours finally', *The Listener*, 1st July 1982.

# Appendix 1

AVERAGE SUNDAY ATTENDANCES IN THE CHURCH OF ENGLAND (1962–1980)

Dioceses                                Rates per 1000 population

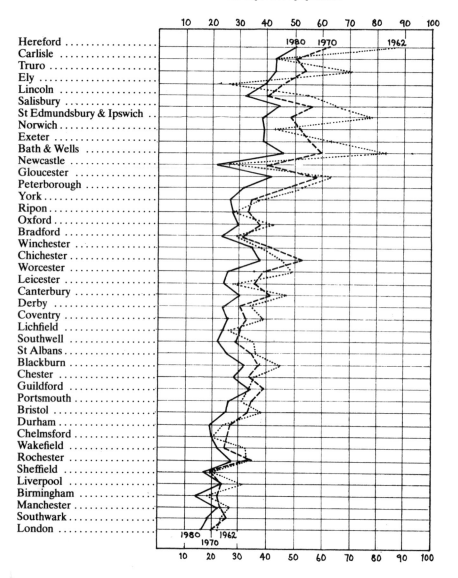

# Appendix 2

FORECAST OF FUTURE NUMBERS OF FULL-TIME DIOCESAN PRIESTS

(Based on varying predictions of the numbers of future ordinations to stipendiary ministry)

*Expected no. of*
*ordinations to*
*stipendiary ministry*

| | | | | | | |
|---|---|---|---|---|---|---|
| 1983 | 340 | 340 | 340 | 340 | 340 | 340 |
| Thereafter | 350 | 340 | 325 | 310 | 300 | 280 |

| *Year* | | | | | | |
|---|---|---|---|---|---|---|
| 1983 | 10,740 | 10,740 | 10,740 | 10,740 | 10,740 | 10,740 |
| 1984 | 10,700 | 10,690 | 10,670 | 10,660 | 10,650 | 10,630 |
| 1985 | 10,670 | 10,650 | 10,620 | 10,590 | 10,570 | 10,530 |
| 1986 | 10,670 | 10,640 | 10,600 | 10,550 | 10,520 | 10,460 |
| 1987 | 10,700 | 10,660 | 10,600 | 10,550 | 10,510 | 10,430 |
| 1988 | 10,750 | 10,700 | 10,630 | 10,550 | 10,510 | 10,400 |
| 1989 | 10,810 | 10,750 | 10,660 | 10,570 | 10,510 | 10,390 |
| 1990 | 10,850 | 10,780 | 10,680 | 10,580 | 10,510 | 10,370 |
| 1991 | 10,900 | 10,820 | 10,700 | 10,590 | 10,510 | 10,350 |
| 1992 | 10,940 | 10,850 | 10,720 | 10,590 | 10,500 | 10,320 |

*Note:* These forecasts have been prepared by the Statistical Unit of the Central Board of Finance and kindly made available to me by Mr Douglas Fryer, Statistics Officer, with the permission of the Ministry Co-ordinating Group. Mr Fryer's figures indicate that a minimum average of 307 ordinations must be achieved each year if the decline in numbers of full-time diocesan clergy is to be arrested.

THE LOCAL CHURCH

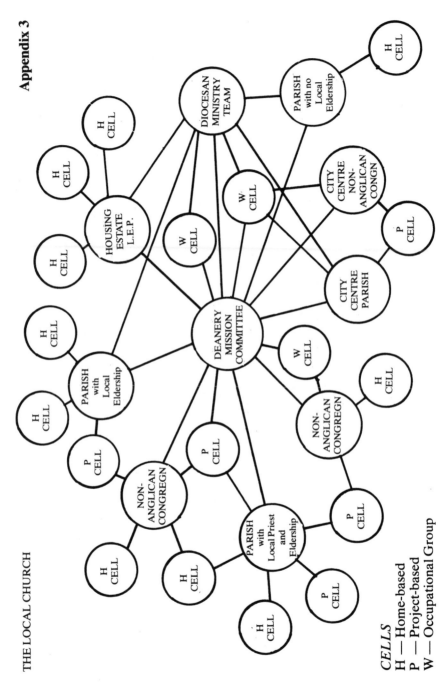

*CELLS*
H — Home-based
P — Project-based
W — Occupational Group

SELECTION AND TRAINING FOR ORDAINED MINISTRY

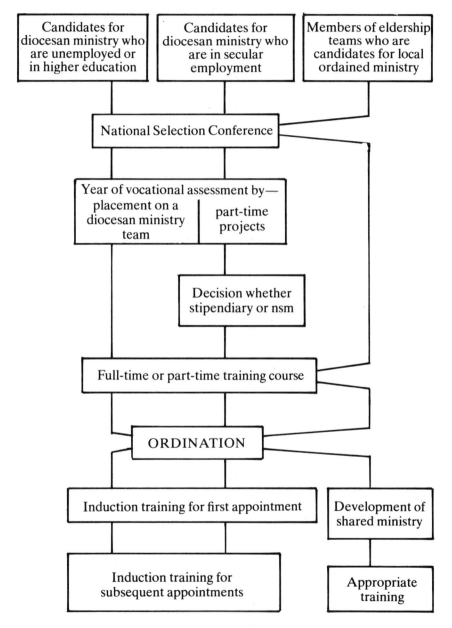

# Select Bibliography

BOOKS

J. A Baker, *The Foolishness of God*, DLT, 1970.
J. M. Barnett, *The Diaconate–A Full and Equal Order*, Seabury Press, N. York, 1981.
D. Bonhoeffer, *Life Together*, SCM Press, ET 1954.
R. Dahrendorf, *On Britain*, BBC, 1982.
R. Denniston (ed.) *Part-Time Priests?*, Skeffington, 1960.
V. J. Donovan, *Christianity Rediscovered: An Epistle from the Masai*, SCM Press, 1982.
M. Gibbs, *Christians with Secular Power*, Laity Exchange Books, Fortress Press, Philadelphia, 1981.
A. D. Gilbert, *The Making of Post-Christian Britain*, Longman, 1980.
R. Gill, *Prophecy and Praxis: The Social Function of the Churches*, Marshall, Morgan and Scott, 1981.
D. Gillett, *How Do Congregations Learn?*, Grove Booklet on Ministry and Worship, No.67, Grove Books, 1979.
M. Green, *Freed to Serve*, Hodder and Stoughton, 1983.
M. Hollings, *Hearts not Garments: Christ is our Peace*, DLT, 1982.
E. James (ed.), *Stewards of the Mysteries of God*, DLT, 1979.
F. R. Kinsler (ed.), *Ministry by the People: Theological Education by Extension*, WCC Publications, Geneva and Orbis Books, Maryknoll, 1983.
B. Martin, *A Sociology of Contemporary Cultural Change*, Basil Blackwell, 1981.
R. Metcalfe, *Sharing Christian Ministry*, Mowbrays, 1981.
P. Moore (ed.), *Bishops–But What Kind?*, Reflections on Episcopacy, SPCK, 1982.
M. Paget-Wilkes, *Poverty, Revolution and the Church*, Paternoster, 1981.
L. Paul, *A Church by Daylight: a reappraisement of the Church of England and its Future*, Macmillan, 1973.
B. D. Reed, *The Dynamics of Religion: Process and Movement in Christian Churches*, DLT, 1979.
K. Roberts, *The Working Class*, Longman, 1978.
A. Russell, *The Clerical Profession*, SPCK, 1980.
E. Schillebeeckx, *Ministry–A Case for Change*, SCM Press, ET 1981.
D. Sheppard, *Bias to the Poor*, Hodder and Stoughton, 1983.
M. Stockwood, *Chanctonbury Ring*, Hodder and Stoughton with Sheldon Press, 1982.

M. Thurian, *Priesthood and Ministry–Ecumenical Research*, Mowbray, ET 1983.
J. J. Vincent, *Into the City*, Epworth, 1982.
J. J. A. Vollebergh et al, *Minister? Pastor? Prophet?*, SCM Press, 1980.
N. Vox, *Monday's Ministries: The Ministry of the Laity*, ed. R. Tiemeyer, Parish Life Press, Philadelphia, 1979.
D. Watson, *I Believe in the Church*, Hodder and Stoughton, 1978.

REPORTS

*The Deployment and Payment of the Clergy*, by L. Paul, CIO, 1964.
*Partners in Ministry:* The Report of the Commission on the Deployment and Payment of the Clergy, CA1640, 1967.
*Ordained Ministry Today–A Discussion of Its Nature and Role*, ACCM, 1969.
*Bishops and Dioceses*, The Report of the Ministry Committee Working Party on the Episcopate, ACCM, 1971.
*First Report of the Terms of Ministry Committee*, GS 87, 1972.
*Deacons in the Church:* The Report of a Working Party set up by the Advisory Council for the Church's Ministry, 1974.
*The Deployment of the Clergy:* The Report of the House of Bishops' Working Group, GS 205, 1974.
*The Theology of Ordination:* A Report by the Faith and Order Advisory Group of the Board for Mission and Unity, GS 281, 1975.
*Alternative Patterns of Training*, GS 265, 1975.
*Theological Training: A Policy for the Future*, A Report by the House of Bishops, GS 303, 1976.
*Koinonia–Diakonia: In search of a relevant community*, An Ecumenical Encounter held at the Centre St Dominique, L'Arbresle, France, 1976.
*Report of the Working Party on the Changing Patterns of the Ministry of Readers*, Ripon Diocesan Readers' Board, 1976.
*The Ministry of Deacons and Deaconesses:* A Report by the Advisory Council for the Church's Ministry, GS 344, 1977.
*Theological Training: A Policy for the Future*, The Guildford Report, GS. Misc. 57, 1977.
*The Second Report of the Working Party on Courses*, GS 359, 1977.
*An Honorary Ministry*, by W. H. Saumarez Smith, ACCM Occasional Paper No.8, 1977.
*The Church of England and Contemporary Communities–*A Working Paper by the Church and Community Unit of the Brunel Institute of Organisation and Social Studies, March 1978.
*The Report of the Lambeth Conference 1978*, CIO, 1978.
*Rural Ministries*, by T. Dorey, Oxford Institute for Church and Society, 1979.

*Tap Roots No.10: Rural Norfolk–Loddon and the Raveningham Group*, BCC, 1980.

*Towards Visible Unity: Proposals for a Covenant:* The Report of the Churches' Council for Covenanting, 1980.

*Shared Ministry, The Report of the Working Party on Ministry made to the Bishop of St Edmundsbury and Ipswich*, December 1980.

*The Continuing Education of the Church's Ministers*, GS Misc. 122, 1980.

*Theological Training for Industrial Ministry*, by T. Elwyn, The Churches' Consortium on Industrial Mission, Recommended Paper Four, 1980.

*On Patterns of Ministry:* The Report of the Ministry Working Party to the Bishop's Council, Diocese of Lichfield, 1980.

*The Church's Ministry–A Survey, November 1980: A Report by the Ministry Co-ordinating Group*, GS 459, 1980.

*Tap Roots No.3: Sherborne Ecumenical Parish*, BCC 1980.

*The Charismatic Movement in the Church of England*, CIO, 1981.

*Life and Death in a Country Church*, by C. Newton, BMU, 1981.

*A Working Paper on the Use of Readers*, Diocese of Southwell Ministry Commission, June 1981.

*Power to the People of God*, a report of the Advisory Council for Training of the Diocese of Birmingham, 1981

*Theological Education in a Multi-Faith Society*, BCC, 1981.

*To a Rebellious House?*, Report of the Church of England's Partners in Mission Consultation, 1981.

*Churches in Urban Priority Areas*, Diocese of Liverpool, 1982.

*A Parish for a Modern City: Southampton Team Ministry, 1973-82*, 1982.

*To Match the Hour*, A Report of a Working Party set up by the Bishops of Liverpool and Manchester, June 1982.

*A Responding Church: A Report on the Finances of the Church of England, 1980-1983*, prepared on behalf of the Central Board of Finance and the Church Commissioners by their Joint Liaison Committee, 1982.

*Baptism, Eucharist and Ministry*, Faith and Order Paper No.111, WCC, Geneva, 1982.

*The Final Report of the Anglican-Roman Catholic International Commission*, CTS/SPCK, 1982.

*Report of a Consultation Concerning the Local Ordained Ministry*, Lichfield Diocese/Shallowford, January 1982.

*Taking Custody of the Future*, by P. Wignall, Oxford Institute for Church and Society, 1982.

*Strategy for Ministry: Report of a Readers' Committee Working Group*, 1982.

*Learning and Teaching in Theological Education*, ACCM Occasional Paper No.11, issued in conjunction with the Board of Education of the General Synod, 1982.

*The Training of Training Incumbents*, ACCM Occasional Paper No.10, 1982.

*Shared Leadership in the Local Church*, by C. Bevington, A Project prepared for a course at St George's House, Windsor, January 1983.

*Episcopacy and the Role of the Suffragan Bishop*, A Report by the Dioceses Commission, GS 551, 1983.

*Appropriate Patterns: An Integrated Strategy for Readers, NSMs, and LNSMs*, by a Working Party of the Bishop's Advisory Council on Ministry, Diocese of Birmingham, 1983.

*Cambridgeshire Villages; A Guide to Local Facilities*, Cambridgeshire Community Council, 1983.

*The Historic Resources of the Church of England: A Report by the Church Commissioners*, GS 563, 1983.

*Episcopacy in the 80s: The Report of a Research-Training Programme for Bishops in the Church of England*, The Urban Ministry Project, The William Temple Foundation, 1983.

*The Financing of Training:* The Report of a Joint Working Party appointed by the Advisory Council for the Church's Ministry and the Central Board of Finance of the Church of England, GS Misc. 175, March 1983.

*Selection for Ministry: A Report on Criteria*, ACCM Occasional Paper No.12, 1983.

*Non-Stipendiary Ministry in the Church of England*, GS 583A, 1983.


ARTICLES

R. Brown, 'Information Technology and the Christian', *Crucible*, Jan.-Mar. 1983.

M. Bourke, 'The Theology of a Non-Stipendiary Ministry', *Theology*, May 1981.

P. Coleman, 'Prospects for the professional ministry', editorial in *Theology*, Nov. 1982.

C. Lewis, 'The Idea of the Church in the Parish Communion', *Crucible*, July-Sept. 1982.

J. Moltmann, 'The Ministry of the Whole Church to the World', *Christian*, vol.6, no.5, Epiphany 1982.

M. Ranken, 'A Theology for the Priest at Work', *Theology*, March 1982.

A. Russell, 'What about the really rural deanery?', *Church Times*, 23 April 1982.

R. Searls, *Journal of the Consultative Conference on the Permanent Diaconate (Ecumenically Considered)*, Distinctive Diaconate Studies, 16, 1981.

G. Stamp, 'Does the Deanery make a difference?', *Crucible*, Oct.-Dec. 1982.

V. Strudwick, 'Local Ordained Ministry: Yesterday's Case for Tomorrow's Church', *Theology*, May 1981.

Sister Teresa, Dss., CSA, *An Exploration of the Diaconate in the Episcopal Church (USA)*, Distinctive Diaconate Studies, 27, 1982.

M. Wharton, 'Pastoral studies in an Anglican theological college', *Contact, The Interdisciplinary Journal of Pastoral Studies*, No.78, 1983.

*The Preface to Crockford's Clerical Directory 1980-82*, Oxford University Press, 1983.

# Index of Main Subjects

173

174